BLACK BELT BUSINESS

The Ultimate Guide

By Matthew Chapman

matthewchapman.online

First Edition

Published in 2023 in the United Kingdom.

Designed by Brazilarte II www.brazilarte.org

CONTENTS

BLACK BELT BIZ	**7**
99 WAYS TO GET A STUDENT	**115**
30 RETENTION STRATEGIES	**183**
MARTIAL ARTISTS GUIDE TO WRITING BETTER COPY	**221**

BLACK BELT BIZ

MORE STUDENTS, MORE PROFIT, MORE FUN!

Black Belt Biz is a manual for struggling Martial Arts instructors. Written by full time Martial Arts Instructor, Author and Business Coach Matthew Chapman, it focuses on how to build a successful and profitable Martial Arts School. Many Martial Arts instructors are frustrated by how difficult it is to grow their school to a point where they can drop their day job and teach Martial Arts full time. This book is written to provide a structured plan that if followed will enable Martial Artists to create a strong stable business that goes from strength to strength.

INTRODUCTION

WHY A BOOK ABOUT THE MARTIAL ARTS BUSINESS?

At the time of writing this book the majority of UK martial arts schools have less than 60 members. This, of course, is OK if you are running your school as a hobby or to share you art. However, if you have set up a martial arts school in order to become a full-time martial arts instructor, having less than 60 students may be a problem. It is very hard to make a living with less than 100 students, unless you charge a premium for your instruction. I usually advise my clients to aim for 100 students as soon as possible because this number of students (if your pricing is right) will allow most part-timers to consider quitting their day jobs and going full-time as a martial arts instructor.

Since the vast majority of schools in the UK have less than sixty students, many instructors are struggling to build their student count. This is why I wrote this book and set up my consultancy at matthewchapman.online. My goal is to help struggling instructors reach that magic 100 student mark, and then move onwards and upwards to 200, 300, and more. Once a martial arts school reaches 100 students great things start to happen. Referrals come in thick and fast, the school's energy increases, the instructor starts to make some money, and things start to take off. This book is packed full of ideas, tips, and tactics that have enabled me to grow my school to over 350 students. Follow my advice, implement the action steps, and you will soon be on the way to creating a successful martial arts business.

WHY YOU MIGHT WANT TO LISTEN TO ME.

My name is Matt Chapman, and I run a successful martial arts academy in Essex, UK. I first started training over 27 years ago and have trained to black belt level in Ninjutsu, Kickboxing, Escrima, and Jeet Kune Do. I am also a Combat Submission Wrestling and Ghost Instructor. I have competed in grappling, kickboxing, and MMA, winning a British Welterweight MMA belt in 2006. So I've been around a bit and done some stuff – big deal.

Since I opened my school, the Masters Academy in 2001 with my training partner James Evans-Nicolle, we have grown our school from zero students to 350 students, and are still growing year after year. We have also done this out of a tiny 1450 sq. ft. industrial unit and have helped set up four affiliate schools, which operate using our syllabus and systems; the largest one has accumulated over 150 members in less than four years.

I tell you this so you understand that we started from nothing and built a successful business that supports both our families and allows us to do what we love to do each day. What more can you ask for? I get up, teach martial arts with my best mate, and that enables me to live a comfortable life.

Believe me, if it's possible for us to do it, then it means you can do it as well. This book will show you how to do it in half the time it took us. We made EVERY mistake possible on our way to running a successful school. When you make so many mistakes it will slow down your growth considerably. However, if you read and implement everything in this book, I see no reason why you cannot achieve more than we have with much less effort and have more fun at the same time.

If you are in the early stages of starting up your martial arts business, you may be experiencing the internal "Shall I, Shan't I" dialogue that can often take place in one's mind.

Common questions you may be asking yourself include the following:

- Will it work?
- What if it goes wrong?
- How do I attract enough students to make a living?
- How do I keep students training with me?

This book is designed to answer all your questions and provide a system to follow that will enable you to build a successful long-term martial arts business.
This book is part business plan, part training manual, and part guidebook. It's written for the person thinking of starting a martial arts teaching business or for someone who currently has a class or school, but is not seeing the results they want.

These poor results may include the following:

- Low student numbers
- High dropout rate
- Little or no profits
- Inconsistent student attendance
- Difficulty retaining senior students

In most cases, these problems can be solved with simple corrective actions. Let's be honest, opening and running a successful martial arts school is not rocket science. It's simply a matter of repeating a few key things day in day out, monitoring the results you get, and making quick changes where appropriate.

Before we get into that, let's look at the ten core principles continually referred to throughout this book.

1. Do what you love
2. Create the type of business you want
3. Choose your niche market
4. Use leverage in everything
5. Funnel vision vs Tunnel vision
6. Testing
7. Efficiency
8. Tenacity
9. People problems
10. Action

So without any hesitation, let's start at number 1.

1. DO WHAT YOU LOVE

I assume that you love martial arts, and that it consumes your waking and sleeping moments. Learning and training fill you with joy, and you devour anything martial arts related with relish. Loving all things martial arts is mandatory if you want to run a successful martial arts school. You are going to need tons of energy and enthusiasm to keep you going, as you overcome hurdles and smash down barriers, especially in the early days!

If you don't truly love martial arts with a burning passion, then maybe a martial arts business is not the best choice for you. Passion will make up for a lot of ignorance and inexperience as you find your feet in the business world.

A burning desire to share the martial arts you love will keep you focused during the good times and bad.

If you can take or leave martial arts, choose something else to do that really lights your fire. You will be doing yourself and your students a disservice by starting a business that you're not truly excited about. The most attractive quality a martial arts instructor can possess is passion. It's infectious, it gets you excited, and it gets your students excited. A passionate instructor inspires and motivates their students to achieve more than they can imagine.

To determine how passionate you are, ask yourself the following questions:

- What do you really like to do (when training)?
- Which do you enjoy more – teaching or training?
- Do you like helping people?
- Do you have lots of patience?
- Do you think about martial arts all the time?
- Do you study martial arts books, videos and websites when you are not training?
- How would you describe your relationship with martial arts?
- In other words, do you have a passion for martial arts?

These questions are designed to get you thinking about how important teaching martial arts is to your happiness. All the skills of an excellent instructor (such as communication, planning and technical skills) can be taught, but a genuine love for what you do cannot be taught or faked. Loving what you do is the most important part of your business success.

However, a word of warning. Most martial arts instructors love to teach and train martial arts, but that's only 30 per cent of being a successful school owner. To be successful, you will have to do a lot of things (at least in the beginning) that you don't enjoy.

In my case, these boring tasks include many aspects:

- Bookkeeping
- Photocopying
- Mopping the mats
- Administration

In the beginning you will have to do all these things yourself. So, although you love the martial arts, there will be a lot of things you have to do that you may dislike. Luckily for you, if your passion for training and sharing martial arts is strong enough, you will do whatever is necessary to see your dream come to life.

As your school gets bigger and you start to earn more, it will be possible to hire people to do the things that you don't enjoy. But, in the beginning, you will have to do everything yourself. Sorry.

2. LIFESTYLE BUSINESS VS. TRADITIONAL BUSINESS

Important distinction: Do you want to create a lifestyle business or build a traditional business? A lifestyle business is exactly what it says: a business you run that allows you to live a certain lifestyle. The classic surfer dude who runs a surf hire shop is running a classic lifestyle business. The surfer makes his or her passion into a job and makes just enough money to maintain a certain lifestyle. They're not looking to build a scalable or replicable business empire, rather they want to enjoy a particular standard of living.

Although they have a business, what they really have is a job. It just happens to be a job they love. My definition of a real business is a profitable entity that continues to grow year on year without you having to be there. If our surfer dude expands, hires staff, opens another shop and starts branding and franchising his chain, he is running a traditional business. Now there is nothing wrong with either way of operating a business as long as you are realistic about what each involves and the commitments needed to make each work.

With a lifestyle business, how you live your life is the primary measure of success. Obviously, the business needs to be profitable to keep your life moving in the direction you want. However, you probably won't want to be working 60+ hours per week, taking out massive loans, or planning on continual expansion.

Most martial arts businesses fall into this lifestyle category and most martial artists dream of teaching for a living in order to:

- Get up when they like
- Potter about, do a bit of work, and drink coffee.
- Do some training every day.
- Have a nap whenever they want.
- Turn up in the early evening and teach a few classes.

Admit it – it sounds pretty good, doesn't it? This is what a lot of martial artists imagine their lifestyle business to be like. Unfortunately, it rarely works out like that because we all have bills to pay and having unpaid bills means you have to work harder. But still, it's a nice dream.

Most of the time, the reality is something more like this:

- Get up early to get your own training done and plan the day.
- Do private lessons throughout the morning.

- Grab a quick lunch.
- Answer calls, emails, etc. in the afternoon.
- Rush to printers to pick up flyers.
- Rush back to teach kids classes from 4 to 6 p.m.
- Teach adult classes from 6 to 10 p.m.
- Clean the academy.
- Go home and eat, answer more emails, do social media, etc.
- Go to bed exhausted.

This is day to day life for many lifestyle business owners. It's kind of cool because you are your own boss and in control of your destiny, but it involves more stress and work than anticipated. There is never enough time in the day, and you are constantly on the go from morning till night. However, if hard work and long hours don't worry you, then it is possible to make a fairly decent living this way. Of course, there is a smarter way.

To run your business like a traditional business requires a totally different mindset. Traditional businesses usually try to grow as fast as possible. This means the business gets bigger and bigger and, ideally, more profitable as it grows. This requires investment, bank loans, business plans, leases, staff, solicitors, partners, and an entirely different set-up. Another common goal of a traditional business is to have a built-in exit strategy. That is, a plan to sell the business at some point. Most lifestyle businesses owners don't think about an exit strategy till they die.

Because traditional businesses aim to grow year on year, they require a different approach. Usually, at some point, the founder stops working in his or her business and hires and trains staff to take over. The owner can then move off the "floor" to a management role, guiding the business as it grows.

To summarise, a traditional business is primarily focused on growth and expansion, whereas a lifestyle business is concerned with maintaining a certain experience for the owner.

Which route you take is based on what you want to do with your life and business. If you want to teach for the rest of your life and want to control everything that happens in your school and don't want to expand, then maybe a lifestyle business might suit you. If you are looking to build a chain of schools or start a franchise that you can manage or sell, then the traditional business model will be preferable.

Of course, these two business models are not mutually exclusive. You could start a lifestyle business, and then move to a traditional business and vice versa. But it is important to have an idea of your goals before you start. This will help you make certain choices on your journey. Do some research, speak to people from both camps, and consider your options.

3. NICHE MARKET

A critical point which goes a long way to determining a business's success is understanding your particular niche market. A niche is a particular segment of the market that you want to work with. For example, some martial arts instructors love working with kids and have a school primarily focused on children's classes. That's their niche market. Other instructors love teaching fighters only, while some schools are adult only and don't cater for children at all.

Below is a list of niches common to martial arts schools:

- Young children (4–5 years)
- Kids (5–10 years)
- Cadets (10–15 years)
- Adults (16 years+)
- Older students (50 years+)
- Ladies only
- Men only
- Fighters
- Fitness fanatics
- Technicians
- Instructors
- Self-defence

Which of these groups are you interested in teaching at your school? It is possible to have all these niche markets training in a single school, but this can lead to a conflict of interests between each group and can make marketing harder. For example, we find that the fitness niche people don't work well with the fighters. Fighters are by nature an intimidating group and can scare off or accidentally injure students from the fitness market.

You need to have a good idea of what particular market/markets you are looking to recruit. This will make your marketing more efficient as it will be more focused and targeted. Instead of trying to catch everyone, you will be able to deliver your marketing message to a specific demographic.

Think carefully about the following questions:

- Which group/groups do you prefer working with?
- Which group/groups do you not enjoy working with?

- If you could have a school full of only one group, which would it be?

Unfortunately, it may not be possible to work with ONLY your preferred niche market, but it can definitely be the focus of your business and marketing. For example, there are several BJJ schools in my local area that are focused on working with elite BJJ athletes. But they also have kickboxing programmes and kids classes in order to fund their preferred niche. You may have to do the same. While we all want to work with our ideal clients, you may need to teach other groups as well to have a profitable business.

Ideal customer analysis

So you know what type of group you would like to work with; the next step is to identify who these people are, where they are, and how to market to them. You do this by creating your "ideal customer".

Ask yourself the following questions:

1. Who is your ideal customer?
2. How old are they?
3. What do they look like?
4. Do they have a family or are they single?
5. Male or female?
6. Profession?
7. Where do they live?
8. What do they do in their spare time?
9. How much disposable income?
10. What do they spend their money on?
11. How do they think about themselves?

By answering these questions, you can create a mental picture of your ideal customer. The person you REALLY want to work with. The more you can get into your ideal customer's head, the easier it will be to market to them as you understand what excites and interests them. And working only with your ideal clients will magnify your passion.

4. LEVERAGE

Leverage is using the minimum force to generate maximum effect. Sound familiar? It should – it's the principle of all martial arts. You will need to become a master of business leverage. As martial artists, we understand how to use leverage whilst training. Now, we need to understand how to use it in business.

Leverage in business is utilised by following these points:

- Using your innate strengths to the maximum.
- Using your time effectively and efficiently.
- Understanding the 80/20 principle and how it applies to business.
- Using other people's time, energy, experience, contacts, and money to help build your business.

By combining leverage correctly, you will maximise your success with less effort and stress.

5. FUNNEL VISION

Funnel vision is a term invented by marketing guru Jay Abraham. He notes that most business owners have "tunnel vision", meaning they do the same as everyone else in their industry.
The problem with this is – if everyone does the same thing, you can get stuck running your business the same way. This may not be the most effective way to run your business, and it may not be the best way for you. But you keep doing it that way because that's how everyone else does it.

Jay prefers to use "funnel vision" where you look outside your industry for ideas and innovations. For example, the direct debit system that many modern martial arts schools use for tuition payment was borrowed from the gym industry. If you look outside your industry, you will find many great ideas that no one else is currently using which can make your business unique and different.

6. TESTING

Testing is simply making sure what you do works. Unfortunately, most martial arts schools don't test or keep statistics, which basically means they don't know what is happening from day to day. You will need to keep accurate statistics on certain key factors that make a major difference in your business.

These key factors are called Key Performance Indicators (KPI). They are the tools that tell you how well you are doing, allowing you to plan and anticipate what will happen in the future.

The KPIs for most martial arts schools include the following:

- Prospect enquiries: the number of people who call, email or drop in to find out about classes as a result of your marketing.

- Intro rate: what percentage of your prospects book onto a trial lesson.
- Sign up rate: what percentage of prospects sign up after the intro lesson.
- Attrition rate: the percentage of students who quit each month.
- Lifetime value: the total amount the average student spends with you over the course of their training.
- Average equipment sales: how much the average students spends on equipment from your pro shop each month.

These are the main KPIs that all martial arts school owners should know. There are many more KPIs, but, for the sake of simplicity, I have kept this list short.

If you track each of these KPIs, it gives you an overview of how your business is performing. It also allows you to notice small issues before they become major problems. Without monitoring these KPIs, you're flying by the seat of your pants, and, before you know it, you can be in serious trouble. Every week, you should run through your KPIs and make adjustments as needed.

Let's say you sit down one week and notice that your sign-up rate has dropped considerably. A little digging may enable you to find out that one of your instructors is having personal problems and is not putting 100 per cent into his intro classes, so prospects are not signing up. In this case, you can change his duties until he is back to normal and have prevented a small problem from becoming something more serious. Monitoring your KPIs allows you to keep a close eye on your business and make quick effective changes.

7. EFFICIENCY

Efficiency is making the most of what you have got. It means maximising leverage and not wasting money, time, or energy. It's very easy to be wasteful in business. You buy things you don't need, waste time on unimportant activities and lose energy in distractions. You increase your efficiency by focusing on the activities that add maximum value to your business. This is known as the Pareto principle – that is 20 per cent of our business activities, bring 80 per cent of the rewards. Not everything is equal in business. Certain things you do will build your business more than others. Let's look at two things a business owner might do in one day.

- Drive to the printer's to pick up flyers.
- Answer enquiries from prospects.

Which of these is more important to your business? It's an obvious example, but hopefully you said answering prospects enquiries, because students bring in the money. Throughout the business owner's day these moments of choice occur frequently. To be efficient, you will have to think clearly and choose the tasks that will have the maximum benefit to your business.

8. TENACITY

Tenacity is the ability to keep going when things get tough. You will encounter many obstacles when running a business. It is vital to have fortitude, so you can keep going and keep thinking clearly when the s**t hits the fan. No matter how careful you are, unexpected things can happen. How you handle these surprises will make all the difference. If you are the type to panic, stress or worry, then you might need to work on building your mental fortitude.

The most important skills to have during a crisis is the ability to keep calm and think logically. So slow down, breathe deeply, and focus on the solution. Too many people focus on the problem during a crisis. This is counterproductive as the problem already exists. Instead, think only about solutions.

There may also be times when running your business that its stability is threatened. It's worth having an emergency plan in place in case of unexpected catastrophe. Let's say your full-time academy floods and is unusable for a few weeks.

Do you have a disaster recovery plan in place?

You should have:

- Money saved for business emergencies.
- Insurance to cover such events.
- A list of alternative venues ready to use.
- Contact details for all your students so you can keep them updated.

9. PEOPLE PROBLEMS

Someone famous once said, "All business problems are people problems." I have a feeling they are right. Most of the problems that I encounter in my business come down to me and my personality. For example, I'm a control freak, so I try to do everything myself, which leads to great inefficiency and stress. Now, I delegate everything that I'm not good at or don't enjoy. I have less control, but I am much happier and more productive.

All of the following personality issues will be magnified in your business:

- Laziness
- Contempt
- Arrogance
- Poor judgment
- Impulsiveness
- Anger
- Indifference
- Lack of empathy
- Control
- Stress

Not that I'm saying you exhibit all of these negative behaviours (not unless you are a serial killer). But there may be one or two that you may have recognised in yourself.

Let's take laziness, for example. I can be very lazy. Unless I have systems in place or have delegated well, some things will not get done. This is an inconvenience in your personal life, but, in your business, it is very dangerous. Bills don't get paid on time, advertising doesn't get done, prospects don't get called back, and before you know it – you are out of business. If I let this character weakness leak into my business, it could ruin me.

Your business is a manifestation of you.
Most problems in your business are problems in yourself.

Let's say you are impulsive by nature. You see a unit you want to rent and convert to a full-time centre. You find out a few cursory details and in a rush of excitement sign the lease and off you go.

Unfortunately, down the line, you find out there are problems with the roof, and the rates are too high. You're not allowed to make any changes to the structure and that promised parking spaces aren't materializing. All these problems could have been addressed before you took on the unit if you hadn't been so impulsive. But you allowed your personality to call the shots.

This means you have to do some work on yourself or at least try to keep your personal problems out of your business life. This is very difficult to do, especially in the beginning where you will be doing everything in your business yourself.

To summarise, you need to take an honest look at yourself and see where your personality may cause problems when running a business. Then put a plan in place to stop yourself from screwing it all up. Do it and you will be ahead of your competition and will save yourself a lot of grief.

10. IMPLEMENTATION

Richard Branson, could tell you how to turn your business into a multi-million pound empire, but if you don't take action nothing will change. There are hundreds of good ideas in this book to help you advertise, increase your student numbers, and earn more money, but, if you read and don't implement, it's all worthless.

You need to get into the habit of taking immediate action when you find a worthwhile idea. If you find something that will improve your business in this book, put the book down, and pick up the phone, or get on the laptop and apply it immediately.

Don't make the mistake everyone else does of thinking, "Wow, that's a good idea, I should do that," and then don't. You have to strike while the iron is hot. Rapid implementation is a key skill in all successful people. If something is worth doing, it's worth doing now!

Make a promise to yourself now that you will implement every time you find an idea in this book that will work for you.

YOUR BUSINESS MISSION STATEMENT

FIRST STEPS: WHY DO YOU DO, WHAT YOU DO?

You need to know why you do what you do as it is at the heart of your business. Your mission statement tells everyone what your business is about: what it stands for, and who it serves. This allows people to get a clear idea about your school, and whether they want to buy from you or not. Some mission statements are long, wordy, and confusing, and some are simple and brilliant.

Starbucks' mission statement captures their essence:

Our mission: *to inspire and nurture the human spirit – one person, one cup and one neighbourhood at a time.*

That's pretty simple and very powerful. You will need to create a mission statement for your business, because it sets the foundation for everything that follows.

Here's how it works:

1. Your mission statement creates your business values.
2. Your values then form your rules and systems.
3. Your rules and systems run your business.

You create a mission statement by thinking about the overall goals you want to achieve and the key qualities you want your business to possess.
My academy's mission statement sums up our values:

To teach fun and informative martial arts in a relaxed, family friendly environment. It tells you what we are all about and what we want to achieve. If you want to train martial arts in a relaxed and fun environment, then we are a great match. If you want a hard/aggressive environment, we're sorry but we can't help you.

So a mission statement sets out your stall and tells the world what you are about. It will turn some people on and some people off, but that is actually a good thing.

BUSINESS GOALS

WHAT ARE YOUR MAJOR BUSINESS GOALS?

You will also need to decide what the major goals for your business are. These goals act as a target to aim for in the next 3–5 years. Of course, these goals will need to be reviewed and changed from time to time, but you need a set of definite concrete goals, so that you can focus and devise a plan to achieve them. Otherwise, you will drift along doing just enough to get by and not push or extend yourself to achieve anything worthwhile. These goals should be BIG goals for your business. Buying a new punch bag is not a major goal. Owning your own 2000 sq. ft. school is a major goal. These goals should scare you a little, as they will force you to grow into the type of person who can achieve them.

My major goals for my business include the following:

- Owning my own 3000 sq. ft school.
- Having ten successful satellite schools under licence.
- Having a team of black belt instructors teaching 90 per cent of the classes for me.

- Running a profitable online University for martial arts school owners.
- Helping small school owners move their business forward via consultancy.

These goals are not small, and they are not easy to achieve. But, that's the point. They will force me to become a better person/businessman in order to achieve them. They will make me grow and expand my comfort zone.

Minor goals

- SMART goals

The next step is to breakdown the major goals into minor short-term goals that will be actionable week by week. We do this by turning our major goals into a series of SMART goals.

SMART is an acronym for these elements:

- Specific
- Measurable
- Achievable
- Realistic
- Timely

Let's take increasing enrolment from 100 to 200 students as an example to see how we would use SMART to get us started.

1. Specific

We want to have 200 active students training within 12 months.

2. Measurable

We would need to get and keep on average nine new students each month to achieve our goal. This does not take into account our attrition rate, of course (attrition is the rate at which you lose students each month). The lower your attrition rate, the better.

The best attrition rate is zero per cent, meaning you don't lose any students. This rarely happens though, as you can't help students who stop because of illness, injury, or work commitments. Successful schools typically have an attrition rate of 2–6 per cent. Any more than that, and you will start having problems growing your school.

3. Achievable

Yes, nine new students per month is achievable if you have an effective marketing system that works.

4. Realistic

It's very realistic. In fact, it may be a little low.

5. Timely

We have set twelve months as our time limit. If we get to six months and haven't hit our targets, then we know we have extra work to do.
Any business goal can be broken down in this way. By breaking it down, it allows you to make a large goal actionable. It's like learning a complex sequence of movements in martial arts. You don't try to learn the whole thing in one go; you split it into manageable chunks.

FULL-TIME OR PART-TIME SCHOOL

Having spoken to many instructors, business owners and management companies, the general consensus seems to be that running classes from halls and leisure centres, rather than having a dedicated full-time studio is the most profitable model for martial arts schools in the UK.

The problem with full-time centres is that, even with a very busy timetable, your gym will be empty and costing you money fully 60 per cent of the time. Even with a timetable that starts at 8 a.m. till 8 p.m., you still have 12 hours every day (the night) where your gym is empty. If your school is empty, it's costing you money in rent and rates.

The advantage of using leisure centres, sports halls, church halls, and scout huts is that you only pay for the time you use. So while the hourly rate is generally high you won't be paying for 12 empty hours every night.

That's not even including a full-time school's problems with business rates, gas and electricity bills, maintenance, and service charges. For most UK martial artists, the full-time model is less cost effective than the renting model. That's not to say you shouldn't get a full-time location, but you will need to think very carefully about the pros and cons before committing yourself. The temptation is to jump in with both feet, as many martial artists long to have their own dojo.

Here are some of the problems with having your own full-time school:

- Rent is due 24/7
- Rates are due 24/7
- Gas and electricity bills
- Cleaning costs
- Security issues
- Equipment depreciation
- Office equipment
- Kitting out reception
- Internet bills
- Phone bills
- Start-up capital
- Tied into a lease/licence

The last one is a major concern. All commercial landlords will want you to sign a licence or lease. This legally ties you to paying rent (and any other costs mentioned in the licence) for the length of the agreement. This means you may have to sign a lease on a building for 5–10 years. This is for both you and your landlord's security.

But what happens if your business fails after three years? Unfortunately, you may still be liable for the remaining rent even if your business has ceased trading. You should only sign a long-term lease if you are very sure of your future earnings, have money saved, have had it checked by a solicitor, and are fully aware of all the risks and commitments involved.

I speak from painful experience. I signed a three-year lease on a space in an office block. After two years of hassles and headaches, we wanted to leave. Luckily, we had a cancellation clause in our lease, but it still meant we had to pay six months' rent on an empty unit we didn't use anymore. Total nightmare. Commercial leases are very tricky and tend to be biased towards the landlord. DO NOT sign one unless you have had professional legal advice.

If you are just starting out, jumping straight into a full-time academy would not be wise anyway. It's just too risky. If you want a full-time place, wait till you have been in business for 3–5 years and have got a few hundred consistent students before taking the plunge. There are, of course, another 50 things to consider before securing a full-time studio which include:

Square Footage. How big a space do you actually need? Unless you have 500 students, anything over 3000 sq. ft. will be unnecessary. Start small and build up slowly. Owning a 10,000 sq. ft. mega facility may seem exciting, but the costs will be astronomical.

Parking. Is there parking for 30–50 cars outside or nearby? If not, how are people going to get to you. Parking is massively important.

Convenience. How convenient is the location? Is it near where you currently offer classes or do your students have to drive 30 minutes out of their way? Is it easy to get to by car, bus, train, and walking? Is it in a high street location or in an out of town warehouse? Is it easy to find?

Proximity to market. Is your chosen location surrounded by your customers? Or is it way out in a field somewhere? Ideally, you want your school to be in or near residential areas.

Appearance. How does it look to the customer's eye? Is the outside attractive, clearly signposted, well lit, and clean? If not, you have a problem. Try not to look at it with your experienced eyes. Look at it as a newbie would, or even better get a friend or relative who hasn't trained in martial arts to give you their honest opinion. It may be a wake-up call for you when they say things like "it looks run down," "it smells in here," "it's a bit dark in the car park."

Security. Is the area secure? Is there security lighting, security patrols, alarm systems, etc.? A safe and secure environment is very important to mums bringing their children to classes, so get this right if you want to teach kids. You will also want to keep your gym equipment secure, as you may have thousands of pounds of stock and kit invested.

Your target market. Are you aiming to recruit young professionals or lots of kids, families, or fighters? Your target market (niche market) will dictate where you locate your full-time school. For example, it will be harder to get families to come to a warehouse-type location on an industrial estate on the outskirts of town. It's not impossible, just harder than having a high street location. Conversely, fighters won't mind where you gym is located and weirdly enjoy a gritty location.

When we were setting up our gym, Masters Academy, we decided on our target market (young professional families), and then got in our car and drove around till we found the perfect location. If you don't live where your ideal market lives, you will have to track them down and open there. Don't expect them to come to you. People tend to stick to their own areas and are reluctant to go places they don't know.

Traffic patterns. In our case, our school is located down a cul de sac. This means we get no passing traffic. Which really sucks. Every person that comes down our road is there for a specific reason and is not just passing by. This means that we cannot rely on passing trade, and therefore have to market more effectively.

Utilities. What does the space include in terms of utilities? Most units have electricity, lighting, toilet facilities, and running water. But you might want to check. Heating is another priority, as is a working phone line.

PRODUCTS AND SERVICES

Martial arts clubs are primarily service-based businesses. In other words, they offer instruction in exchange for money. This will obviously form the foundation of your income, but there are many other physical and informational products you can offer to top up your income.

First, you will need to decide which classes you are going to offer and how you will organise timetabling. Let's look at common groups of customers and suitable timetables for them.

Young children 4–5 years

This age group can usually only concentrate for short periods, so at our school we only teach them for 30 minutes. If it's any longer, the kids get distracted and lose focus. The classes are fun-based and develop balance, co-ordination, strength, focus, and discipline, the martial arts emphasis is kept fairly low. We usually run these classes directly after schools close, so 4 p.m. is a good time to start. This allows parents time to come straight from school to the academy.

Older children 6–9 years

This group has a better ability to concentrate and stay focused. These classes are usually 45 minutes long, and have more of a martial arts emphasis. They usually follow the younger kid's class after their session ends at 4.30 p.m.

Cadets 10–15 years

This group is capable of learning most techniques and training for at least an hour. We usually teach a full martial arts syllabus with lots of fitness integrated to burn off excess energy. These classes typically start at 5.30 p.m.

Ladies only

We have a large number of women training at our school. Some are working women, and some are stay at home mums. The mums seem to prefer late morning classes, since they can drop the kids off at school and come straight to training. We run classes for these women at 9.30 a.m. We also offer dedicated women only classes in the evening from 7.30 p.m. for those that work.

Shift workers

We run a few classes each week for shift workers. Based on their shifts, sometimes they can make the morning sessions, and sometimes they can make evening ones.

We have 9.30 a.m. classes and 9 p.m. classes for this group.

Adults

Many adults who work, prefer to come straight from work and like to train at 6 p.m. Other people would rather go home first, freshen up, and then come to class. We cater for them with classes at 7–8 p.m. The main focus of these classes is on fitness and grading-based martial arts.

Weekenders

Some people are too busy in the week to get to training, so we offer a few classes on Saturdays for these students. These classes are usually very well attended. You may also consider opening on Sundays to allow the maximum amount of traffic through the weekend.

Open mats

At quiet times of the day, it is useful to offer open mat sessions. This is where students come and do their own training. You need to be there to monitor what's going on, but essentially they are left to get on with it. This is a productive time for students who want to drill or spar. Typically open mats run between 12 noon and 4pm.

By offering a wide variety of classes, you maximise your potential market.

REVENUE STREAMS

There are numerous sources of revenue when running a martial arts school.

CLASS FEES

These will be your main source of income. There are five ways most martial arts schools accept payment for classes.

1. Cash per class.

This is usually the least preferable way to get paid. The problem with cash per class is that if your student is ill and doesn't turn up, you don't get paid. If your student leaves work too late and can't make training, you don't get paid. If your student is tired and stays at home instead, you don't get paid. This method of collecting fees leaves you vulnerable to random external events affecting your cash flow. For example, if there's an important football match on a certain night, your class size could halve. That's bad for business.

2. Monthly cash payment.

To counter the problems associated with cash per class, many martial arts schools charge fees monthly. Students pay a fee for one month's training in advance. This works better than accepting cash per class as it guarantees you will get paid for that particular month.

The problems with accepting monthly payments are that you are constantly chasing students for money. They forget to bring it or haggle with you ("ah, but I missed all of last week, can I pay less this month"). Using this payment method, you will constantly feel like a debt collector, hassling your students for money. Still, it's better than being paid per class.

3. Cash outs

If you are certain of being in an area for a long time, and you have good money management, you could also consider cash outs. This is offering a special rate for students who pay for 12 to 24 training months in advance. Usually schools offer a discount of 10–25 per cent to students who cash out. This can prove quite popular, as some people love a sweet deal or would just rather pay for training in advance.

This is also a good way to quickly raise some capital if you need to get a deposit together, or have to buy a large piece of equipment (such as a ring or MMA cage). The main problem with cash outs occurs if you cash out too high a percentage of your student base. You will then significantly reduce your monthly income. This can be a problem if you don't manage the lump sum you received. It's common for instructors who have cashed out 50 per cent of their school to turn up to class in a shiny new sports car.

Unfortunately for them, bills still need to be paid, and, if they haven't set aside sufficient savings for expenses and unexpected bills, cash outs can get you into trouble. It is, therefore, advisable to not cash out more than 10 per cent of your school. This way you get a nice injection of cash when you need it, but still retain a steady monthly cash flow.

4. Standing orders

Some schools get their students to pay via a monthly standing order in an attempt to automate payment. The problem with standing orders is that the student is in complete control of the payments. They have to set it up, make any changes, and can cancel it without informing you. Even getting the student to set up a standing order can be difficult in the first place. They frequently forget to do it, so you have to chase them. Then if they upgrade their training and want to increase their standing order, they have to cancel the old one first, to set up a new one. What a hassle for them. And finally they can just go to their bank and cancel it without informing you.

This means if you are not constantly monitoring your payments, they may be able to train for free for a few months before you find out. A better choice than standing orders is a direct debit.

5. Direct debit (DD)

The best option for the long-term stability of your business is to get students to sign a direct debit mandate for their training fees. This means a student's fees are deducted from their bank account monthly. This automates the whole process of getting paid. To benefit from using direct debit, you will need to sign up to a billing company. This is an external company that manages your payments and accounts for you. For this service, they usually charge anything from 6–10 per cent of the fees collected. Now, this may seem like a lot to give up, but they take all the hassle out of getting paid.

You sign up with them, and they send you the direct debit forms for your students to complete. It's then a simple matter of posting off the completed direct debit forms each week. The billing company will also chase non-payers and late payments and send them a letter reminding them to pay. This allows you to focus on what you should be doing, teaching martial arts, and building your business. The company I use is called NEST Management and is, in my opinion, the best in the UK for their services and innovations. I have tried several others, but NEST provides the best customer service and support.

Once a student is signed up, they need to make sure they have the training fees in their account on the day you want to collect them. If the money isn't there, NEST will write to them and tell them that it will try to collect again a few days later. If that doesn't work, NEST will email you, telling you who hasn't paid and why. You can chase them up yourself and take payment at your school, or let NEST deal with it.

This is definitely worth the 6–10 per cent they charge as it makes your life a whole lot easier.

So if you haven't opened your school yet, it's worth starting with DD payments if possible. We started our first classes at a David Lloyd Gym in 2001 and, within a few months, had students signed up on DDs. If, however, you have a school where students pay cash currently, set a date when you will be changing to DDs. Let your students know in advance, and give them the option to cash out for the rest of the year. Cashing out means they get to pay for the rest of the year in cash, and then start a DD in the New Year.

Unfortunately, once you start transferring students from cash to DDs you may get some resistance and may lose a few stubborn students. But, as long as it's handled gently, it usually works out OK with the majority of customers. Just be nice, explain why the change is needed, and help people out where you can.

WHAT TO CHARGE FOR YOUR CLASSES

Martial arts consultants and billing companies are always advising schools to raise their prices. This is because of the high value students get from martial arts training, and the fact that the majority of clubs are still not charging enough. When I started training almost thirty years ago, a martial arts class cost £2.50 and a can of coke was 20p. Now the can of coke is £1–2, yet some schools are still charging £2.50 per class. This is a problem as it devalues what we are all offering and makes it difficult to earn a living for professional instructors.

As you know, martial arts offers a host of benefits to its practitioners including the following:

- Fitness
- Weight loss
- Stress release
- Self-defence skills
- Self confidence
- Fun
- Meeting cool people
- Variety
- Social events
- Focus for children
- Guidance and advice
- Absorption in training
- Instruction and motivation in every class

This is worth way more than £2.50 per hour. In America, it's quite common for schools to charge $150–$300 a month. And, of course, the UK is always 10 years behind the US. At the time of this writing, most church-hall-type instructors charge between £2.50–£7 per class and most full-time schools charge from £5–£20 per class. Saying that, there is no reason why a church hall operation can't charge closer to £20 a class. It all depends on the value you deliver, your marketing, and your target niche market.

It's always easier to start prices high and lower them if you need to, rather than start too low and try to increase them. You will have a battle on your hands if you decide to raise your prices. So if you haven't set your prices yet, find a price you are comfortable with and then double it. Seriously, if you were thinking of charging

£5 per class, charge £10. You can lower you price if needed, but if you demonstrate amazing value to your students and ask for it in a confidently, you may be surprised how many people will join.

If you think you have set your prices too low, then you have a choice. Raise the prices of your classes or raise the prices of your add-ons (or preferably do both Add-ons are things like gradings, equipment, and seminars. Students tend not to worry about a price increase in something they only do occasionally (like take a grading), but naturally they get very worked up about an increase in something they pay weekly or monthly.

If you are going to raise your prices for your classes (as you probably should), you should give people plenty of warning (of at least a few months) before the price increase will take effect. No one likes surprises, especially a sudden increase in expense, so pre-warn them. I also recommend you explain why the prices are increasing. Write a letter to be given to all students and parents, explaining why the prices have to increase. Rising costs, inflation, rates, renovations, new equipment purchases, new classes, and extra training all cost you as a business owner more money. These costs have to be passed onto the student or eventually you will go out of business.

Gently explain why a price increase is necessary, and tell students that anyone can speak to you if they have problems affording the new price. A small percentage will come forward, so do your best to help them out by offering a discount for a specific time frame. You could also offer them the chance to pay for the rest of the year in a lump sum at the "current rate before the increase in prices." That way if you increase the prices in June, they can pay for the rest of the year at the reduced rate as long as they pay the six months in advance.

Only do this if you have good money management skills. It will be tempting to buy a new gadget with all the extra money coming in. Remember you may owe a lot of students six months training, so be disciplined with your money.

OTHER SOURCES OF INCOME IN A MARTIAL ARTS BUSINESS

PRIVATE LESSONS: £40-200 PER HOUR

Many students request private instruction to help achieve specific goals. Private lessons are very popular with adults looking to improve fitness or work towards a specific target, such as a belt grading. The main problem with privates is finding the space to do them and charging appropriately. If you run a full-time centre, then scheduling private lessons is easily done during quiet times. If you teach out of a leisure centre, then you can either do privates at your client's home (with awareness of certain insurance and safety issues). Or, many instructors teach privates outside in parks during spring and summer. The explosion in bootcamps means people are more comfortable training outside these days.

If you don't have a dedicated space, then consider offering training outside. Just be aware that some local parks and spaces may not be willing to let you use their space to earn money. Do your research and find local public spaces you can use for free.

Depending on how you position your skills and expertise, you can charge anything from £40–200 per hour. If you think of certain celebrity fitness coaches, they routinely charge many hundreds of pounds an hour by positioning themselves as a trainer to the stars. Obviously, this takes a lot of work in developing your brand and exposure, but it is possible.

At the other end of the scale is the training of "regular" folk. Typically, you should be getting paid from £40–80 an hour for private instruction (more if you have to travel).

If you don't enjoy doing privates and aren't that bothered, then charge £60–100 an hour. You will only get a few people interested at that rate, but you will earn well when someone books a session.

Personally, I prefer to do group privates where I get two to four people to do a private at the same time. The benefit to them is they get a cheaper lesson and, conversely,

I earn more per hour. For example, I would charge a group of four students £100 for an hour, so they each pay £25. This works if you have a group of friends who want to train together. Or, if you are fully booked with single privates, you could make all future privates small groups only. Thereby requiring students to bring their friends if they want semi-private instruction.

One further advantage of group privates is that it saves you wear and tear on your body. Training with students, holding pads, and grappling are OK if you only have two or three a week. But if you have ten individual privates a week, it can start to deplete you, leading to injury and illness.

If you are getting overwhelmed with privates, tell your students gently that you are over-subscribed, and that they will have to share from now on. Most students will understand and oblige. Plus it works out to be cheaper for them and is less stressful for you.

If you want short-term cash, you can also offer private block bookings. For example, book ten privates and get two free. Or have students pay in blocks of 20, 30, or 50 lessons. Yes, some people will fork out a couple of grand on privates if they get a good deal. All you have to do is ask, and the worst that will happen is that they will say no.

SEMINARS £20–100 PER PERSON

Seminars prove popular if marketed/promoted well by instructors. They are usually on different subjects than your normal syllabus. This makes them novel and interesting, which creates a bit of excitement or you can hold seminars focused on a particular part of your syllabus (kicking, for example). Seminars can be technique focused, such as learning a certain style. They can be fitness focused as on burning calories and having a "workout," or they can be performance focused as in, "10 ways to punch harder."

The secret with seminars is to give people plenty of lead-up time to book it into their diary. Then spend the 4-6 weeks leading up to the seminar creating a buzz about it.

Teach some of the seminar material in your classes, post YouTube clips of the style that you will be teaching. Talk it up on your Facebook page, and get people excited about it.

PAID INTRO COURSE OR FREE TRIAL?

Most martial arts schools offer a free trial class to allow students to try out their services before they commit. We used to offer in our crazy days 30 days free training.

This was one offer that differentiated us from the competition. Unfortunately, it became unmanageable as it was hard to track people over the course of a month. Now, we offer one week's free training to new students. This allows them to try out a range of classes, and, if they return the following week, we know they are ready and willing to sign up. Really the length of the free trial is up to you. One class is generally the minimum trial, or you can offer more based on what is fair and profitable.

Many schools have done away with the free trial and now require prospects to book onto an intro workshop to learn the fundamentals. These workshops are typically 3–6 weeks long and schools charge anything from £20–99 for attendance. The advantage for the business owner is that they get paid while the prospect tries out their services. You can add lots of free giveaways (T-shirts, reports, DVDs) to the deal to make these paid intros more appealing to new prospects. The only way to see which method (free trial vs. paid intro) works best for your business is to try both approaches for a period of time and see which is most effective at attracting and converting new prospects.

THE PERFECT INTRO CLASS

Once you have done your marketing and attracted a new person to your school, here's what you should NOT DO first:

Don't leave them hanging at the door isolated and scared.
Most new students are, to use a technical term, "shitting themselves." They are worried they are going to get beaten up, injured, or made to look like a fool. Prospects are always nervous about their first class, and they should be. There are still martial arts gyms that see new students as "fresh meat" to be devoured.

Admittedly, these clubs don't have many members, but they create a bad impression for more professional clubs.
We have all heard horror stories of first-time students sparring with professional fighters and getting beaten up. In what way does that benefit either the new student or the fighter? What it does is turn the new student off martial arts for life, and when anyone mentions doing martial arts to them they say, "Don't do it, I got beaten up, it's full of nutters."

So, when our new student has finally plucked up the courage to come, do you leave them hanging by the door for five minutes while you finish a class? I tell you what happened to me once when I did this, they prospect walked straight back out the door. They feel vulnerable, scared, and alone, getting more and more worked up and think "Screw this, I'm outta here."

As soon as you see a newbie at the door – make eye contact, smile, stop what you are doing (if possible) walk over, and say "hello" warmly. Problem solved. Then give them something to do while they wait for their class to start. All new students should fill in a PAR-Q, which is a pre-activity readiness questionnaire. This helps you to check if they are healthy and OK to train.

You'd be surprised how many people turn up to a class with a pre-existing serious injury. We even had one guy try to start training after he had just had a broken neck!

By filling out a PAR-Q, you are essentially covering yourself if anything should happen during the first class, and you are giving the new student something to do while waiting. People rarely tell the truth on these forms anyway, but that's not the point.

If they say they are fit to train and injure themselves because of a pre-existing injury that they didn't tell you about, you are OK as long as you weren't negligent in some way. Make sure all new students fill in a PAR-Q, and then keep it for at least three years.

CHUCKING THEM INTO A CLASS ALONE

A lot of schools just drop newbies into a class, and let them fend for themselves. Classic sink or swim! This is definitely not the best idea. Most professional schools run group intro classes to which all beginners can come. The other option is the semi-private intro where the newbie is introduced into the regular class, but mentored by a senior student or instructor, who will help them and train with them for their first class. Which method you choose is up to you and will depend on the numbers in your class, timetable space, and the number of assistant instructors available to help. What you don't want to do is chuck them in at the deep end without some support. Several bigger schools also do private intro sessions with an instructor and the newbie only. If you have the ability to do it, this method is considered the most successful conversion method of all. It helps personalise the session and starts building a relationship.

Trying to teach newbies everything you know about martial arts in one session. I used to be guilty of this. I so wanted to share my passion for martial arts that I would try to teach them everything I knew in one lesson. As a result, they felt overwhelmed, didn't learn anything, and got frustrated. The result is a lost student.

We now make all our instructors teach a very basic first lesson to the new students

Here is a sample lesson plan for a prospects trial lesson.

KICKBOXING	BJJ	MMA
Warm-up Stance Front kick Jab-cross Knee Blend all 3 Stretch	Warm-up Guard Grips & posture in guard Basic opening guard Rolling (Try to open guard-reset) Stretch & watch rolling	Warm-up Guard Grips & posture in guard Basic opening guard Rolling (Try to open guard-reset) Stretch & watch rolling

KICKBOXING
Stance Front kick Game Straight knee Game Drink Jab- cross Game Mix all three in combo: Front kick – jab – cross – knee Award white belt at end of first session

As you can see the lesson plan for each group is very basic. The idea is to give them a simple, positive experience. They should work on their fitness, learn a few basic techniques and have fun. If they are knackered, sick, confused, and stressed, are they likely to come back for more? Probably not, but I still see instructors beasting new students with loads of burpees or confusing the hell out of them with complex drills and combos. No, No, No. Keep It Super Simple. They should learn one or two basic techniques, break a sweat, but not too much, and have a bit of a laugh. If you can do that, then they will come back for more.

Also make sure newbies also get plenty of rest breaks and water stops to recover. Being too serious Martial arts is full of serious people, looking mean and acting tough. If you went into Curry's to buy a TV and the assistants looked mean and acted tough you would complain about their attitude. What makes the martial arts industry so different?

We are providing a service and in the service industry you should be approachable, open, and happy to help. People like to spend time and money with relaxed and helpful people.

If you can help your newbies to laugh and have fun they will relax and begin to open up to you. Obviously, this doesn't mean going down to the pub with them after training. It means just using humour and grace to diffuse the tension they feel about coming to your scary gym. Unfortunately, I have been training for 28 years, so I can't remember how it feels to be a nervous beginner. Occasionally, I go to a seminar or go to a different gym, and I do get a little nervousness, especially when I'm teaching my Mitt Master pad striking system to a new group. But I don't get "beginner" nervous, so although I can kind of understand how newbies feel, I'm (and you are) too experienced to fully appreciate the state they can work themselves into. Be gentle and supportive. A little TLC works wonders with new students.

Matching them up poorly

Always match like with like. This means if you have an overweight woman, try to partner her with another woman and preferably one that is overweight as well. Since they are physically similar, they will feel more relaxed and comfortable rather than being partnered with a ripped 20-year-old man for example. The super-fit young man also needs to be paired with another super-fit young man as they will most likely enjoy working together.

Here are some things you should try to match.

- Age
- Gender
- Weight
- Height
- Experience
- Temperament

All of those are self-evident really. It's probably not safe to have a 20-year-old working with a 60-year-old for example. But a lot of instructors forget matching temperaments.

Hot-headed people should be matched with other hot-heads. These types like to compete, work hard, and spar harder. If you put one of these aggressive hot-heads with a shy, introverted "cool" type of a person, it will scare the pants off the introvert.

Remember, people like people like themselves. That's why people form cliques in any social situation. The geeks hang with the geeks, the sporty types hang with other sporty types, and so on. Match students well at the beginning of class, and you will make your life a whole lot easier. If you can't find a match for someone, that's what punch bags are for. Put them on a punch bag and swap them in with another matching group regularly.

Only using your black belt eyes

Martial Arts maverick John Graden invented the term "black belt eyes." You look at your gym with black belt eyes not with novice eyes.

This is how a black belt sees their gym:

1. The sweaty odour is a good sign of hard work and dedication.
2. The blood-stained punch bags show that this is a hardcore gym.
3. The pile of stinky old boxing gloves shows that we have been doing this for ages.

Here's how a newbie interprets the same things:

1. "Wow, it stinks in here. I think I'm going to be sick."
2. "Is that blood on those bags? Holy crap, that's really unhygienic."
3. "Does he really want me to put my hands in those stinking old gloves?"

That's the difference between black belt eyes and normal eyes. The best thing you can do to cure this affliction is get a non-martial artist to come to your school, and honestly tell you their opinion about what they see, smell, and touch.

If they are honest, they will say things like:

1. "It smells of feet in here" (so you need to clean daily, use air fresheners and throw out all old kit).
2. "The walls are dirty" (needs a fresh coat of paint).

3. "There is blood on the bags" (make sure you clean the bags every day).
4. "These gloves smell rank" (throw them out and buy washable neoprene gloves).
5. "The floor is dirty" (clean and mop daily).
6. "It's a bit gloomy in here" (clean windows and boost artificial lighting).

After this exercise, you should get a list of 20–50 things you can improve to make your gym more beginner friendly. This is important because first impressions make a big difference. For example, when our club gloves start to stink, we throw them out and buy new ones, and we also have hand sanitizer available for people to use.

We also buy neoprene gloves, which you can wash in a regular washing machine to help keep them fresh. To us seasoned martial artists, smelly gloves are just part of the fun, but for newbies it really puts them off.

LETTING THEM WALK OUT THE DOOR WITHOUT CAPTURING THEIR DETAILS OR DISCUSSING THEIR EXPERIENCE

First things first. People won't tell you the truth. You are an authority figure, and people will tell you what they want you to hear. Although internally they are thinking "That was awful," they will tell you they loved every second and will be back next week. Don't stress, it just is what it is. But, at least you need to make sure you capture their name, email address, and mobile number. You need these things, so you can continue to converse with them after their trial class and hopefully convert them. Usually the day after their trial session, I send all newbies a text message along these lines:

> *We hope you enjoyed your first class at Masters Academy. If you have any questions or need any help, please get back to us at any time.*
> *We look forward to seeing you at your next free session on ...*
>
> Thanks,
> Matt Chapman
> Masters Academy

Why do we do this? Because it builds a bridge between you, starts a conversation, and shows you care, which is very rare in today's world. Do you get a text message from Starbucks after you have bought your Mocha-latte- frappucino? No, you don't, so we stand out in our prospect's mind for making the effort. Usually, most people reply and confirm when they will come back. This one thing, which takes ten minutes at the end of the day, makes a massive difference to your sign-up rate. Do it from now on.

JOINING FEES

Most martial arts clubs charge a joining fee. It is usually to pay for insurance and registration, but it should also cover your marketing costs. If you pay £100 to advertise on Facebook, and you get five people to join as a result of your advertising, each person has cost you £20 to acquire. The joining fee should cover all of your marketing expense plus insurance and any other associated costs.

You can calculate how much it costs you on average to acquire a student, and can set your membership fees to cover that acquisition cost and make a profit as well. But, of course, you need to calculate your acquisition cost first. More on this later.

Many schools charge a yearly membership fee. I personally think this is a good idea and can add a massive boost to your profits every January when you renew your entire school. However, it all depends on how your clients feel about paying a renewal fee every year. As our school started with a one-off payment, it would be nearly impossible for us to introduce a yearly renewal without alienating the entire school and, probably, losing a lot of students. If you are starting afresh, then a yearly renewable membership will make your business far more lucrative.

In the end, what you charge as a membership fee is a personal choice, but it's good to be flexible and offer a range of packages to suit every budget.
For example, we offer the following membership options.

Bronze membership

- Lifetime academy membership
- Academy T-shirt
- Academy members website access

Silver membership

- Lifetime academy membership
- Academy T-shirt
- Academy members website access
- Bag gloves

Gold membership

- Lifetime academy membership
- Academy T-shirt

- Academy members website access
- Boxing gloves
- Focus mitts
- Training DVD

Some people prefer the bronze, others go for the gold, but most choose the silver. That's how people work. If you have three options or prices, most people choose the middle option. Weird, but true.

EQUIPMENT SALES

All professional schools have a pro shop that offers a variety of martial arts supplies to the students. This ensures students have access to good quality equipment which will improve their training and also boosts the schools income.

You can expect to make 50–100% profit on most items in a pro shop. All you need to do is apply for a trade account with a few local and national martial arts suppliers. They will usually ask for proof of your grade and maybe your website address to check that you operate a school. Once they have this info, you can buy equipment from them at trade prices. It's not uncommon for the bigger schools to earn an extra £1–5K per month from their pro shop.

Obviously your pro shop should benefit your students by giving them access to high-quality equipment at prices cheaper than retail. Otherwise, your students will buy cheap and dangerous equipment off the Internet. It's better for them and better for you to get everything they need in-house. To encourage your students to get the equipment they need, you can make certain items a requirement for particular grades or classes.

For example, we require our Orange belts (second grade) to own a pair of boxing gloves before they can go for their next belt. This stops them from using our sometimes stinky club gloves and means that they are more likely to keep training since they have invested in their own training. We have required equipment for every grade, from white belt to black belt. This includes:

- Club uniform
- Boxing gloves
- Focus mitts
- Groin guard & gum shield
- Shin guards
- Thai pads

This is the essential equipment you would expect to see in any kickboxing black belt's kit bag. Having "required equipment" might appear a bit manipulative to some, but the fact remains that to do any sport you need the right kit. If you take up football, you are expected to buy your own boots, shin guards, and club kit. There is no difference for martial arts. To get the best from their training, all martial artists use equipment to facilitate their training. It just means if they buy it from you, the quality, safety, and a fair price is guaranteed.

Plus some of the cheap equipment on the market is dangerous. Poor quality padding, bad stitching, and sharp labels have been responsible for a number of nasty injuries recently. We have even banned a certain cheap equipment brand that is popular right now precisely because of how unsafe it is. If students don't want to buy your kit, suggest some high-quality alternatives, but don't let them use dangerous equipment.

Try to introduce new items regularly to boost sales. As manufacturers come out with new products, add them to your pro shop. For example, a company called Fresh Gloves started selling charcoal glove deodorisers. Right now, they are one of the most popular items in our shop, as they stop boxing gloves from stinking. So keep an eye out for new products that you think will sell.

One of the most important considerations with running a pro shop is how much stock to hold. Obviously, you don't want to have a lot of money tied up in stock that you can't sell, but you should have key items in stock at all times. In our kickboxing club, we make sure we always have T-shirts, boxing gloves, and gum shields in stock. For more exotic items, we order in when people want them, as most suppliers can get kit to you within 48 hours.

Finally, make sure you get paid before you order a student's kit. Several times we have had people order over £100 of equipment and then they decide that they don't want it. Brilliant. We now make sure everyone pays in advance before we order.

Make it an unbreakable rule to that students pay in full before you order.
A great tip if you need to make some money quickly is to do a sale or return special event. This is where you go to a local martial arts supplier (with whom you have a good relationship) and take some stock on sale or return, meaning whatever you don't sell, you return to the shop. In this way, you can run a sale at a moment's notice and return any equipment you don't sell. At the last sale we did, we made £750 profit in one hour, so it's definitely worth investigating.

Another important issue when considering pro shop sales is how easy it is for people to pay. For over eight years, we didn't have a debit card machine. Major mistake. No one carries cash anymore. Students, who wanted to buy a piece of equipment, would pull out their debit/credit card, and we had to say, "Oh sorry, we don't have a machine, can you bring the cash next week." Sometimes they did, but most of the time they forgot – which equals a lost sale.

The best decision we made was to get a PDQ machine (credit or debit card payment machine). To get one cheaper, we joined the Federation of Small Businesses as they offered a PDQ machine at a cheaper rate than if you used your bank. If you operate out of school halls, you can get one like we have that works via mobile phone signals. All you do is put a special SIM card in the back, and you are ready to take card payments wherever you can get a phone signal. No phone line required.

Using a card machine makes payments simple, easy, and quick. Everyone carries cards but only a small percentage of people carry cash regularly. Also, there is a big psychological difference between handing over a fistful of cash versus handing over your card. It's always easier for people to spend using their cards. We also accept cheques and cash, of course. But 80 per cent of the time we get paid via cards.

In the first month we had the machine, we took an extra £600 in orders. So it paid for itself and more within one month.

Make sure you have your most popular items in stock at all times. People get excited about buying their first pair of gloves, for example, and feel disappointed when they have to wait two weeks for them. Plus, they can try them on and get a feel for them which helps them to commit to buying. Work out your five most popular pieces of equipment and make sure you always have several in stock.

EQUIPMENT PACKS

It is also worthwhile creating equipment packs that you can offer students. We have a striking pack, a boxing pack, a sparring pack, and a weapons pack.

The striking pack includes:

Bag gloves

Focus mitts

Glove deodorisers

Pad training DVD

The boxing pack includes:

Boxing gloves

Hand wraps

Gum shield

Skipping rope

The sparring pack includes:

16 oz. boxing gloves

Shin guards

Groin guard

Gum shield

The weapons pack includes:

A pair of eskrima sticks

Training knife

Soft sparring stick

Protective goggles

Gloves

These packs are suitable for different groups in your school. By buying a training pack, they are psychologically committing to a programme and are more likely to stick with it because they have committed their money. Always make a pack slightly cheaper than buying the items individually. This is what makes them attractive to your students as it saves them money.

The types of packs you offer are only limited by your imagination. You could include a "Prestige Pack with Deluxe Equipment" or a "Muay Thai Pack with Thai Pads, Belly Pad, and Shorts." Experiment with different packs and see which prove popular with your students.

PRODUCT OF THE WEEK

Always have a product of the week. It is displayed centrally in your display and changes each week. If you let your students know that there will be a special deal available each week, they will keep an eye out each week. Everyone likes a special deal.

GET HELP OR DO IT ALONE? CONSULTATION

It may be worth getting help with your business as you will make a lot of mistakes in your first few years, before you work out what the hell you are doing. These mistakes will cost you time, energy, money, and stress. You can either learn these things the hard way or use other people's experience to help you avoid unnecessary suffering.

There are many companies and individuals who offer coaching or consultancy services. I, for example, have a part of my business where I work one-on-one with small-school owners to help them grow to the next level. You can check out my business coaching website here: matthewchapman.online. Or, you can choose one of the bigger billing and tuition companies such as NEST. We use them to collect our tuition fees, but they also offer detailed marketing plans, systems, and excellent training on how to run a successful school. They are also always on the end of the phone if you want advice or support. Their customer service is second to none. We have been using them for over a decade, and they always add value and help us out.

Once you have your school up and running, the next step will be about optimisation and innovation. You will need to make sure all your processes and systems are working at an optimal level. Everything from marketing through to teaching classes will need to be structured, tested, and refined. Once you have optimised and got the best from what you are currently doing, the next thing to consider is innovation. Innovation means coming up with creative solutions to common problems or finding ways of improving what is already working.

Innovation happens when you expand your mind and start learning from various other businesses around you. The problem with any industry (including the martial arts industry) is everyone does the same as everyone else. You do what your instructor did and so on. It's part of the traditional nature of martial arts, and, while it's admirable in terms of learning a style, it can be a hindrance in business. You will have absorbed a whole raft of opinions and attitudes about the martial arts business from your instructor. Some of their opinions will be helpful, and some will hold you back from achieving your potential.

To give you an example, there are still instructors out there who believe that it's immoral to make money from teaching martial arts. If you have been taught by one of these instructors, you will have absorbed their attitude to money and martial arts and will feel a lot of resistance to charging for your services. In order to get paid what you deserve, you will have to overcome your instructor's voice in your head, telling you that you are a "sell out." This is incredibly difficult to achieve, especially, if you are still in contact with the instructor. This is where a business coach can help by giving you an impartial viewpoint.

Other common traditional attitudes about the martial arts business include the following:

- Not charging for belt gradings.
- Not wanting to grow your school in order to maintain the quality of your students.

- Not awarding belts till students have demonstrated ridiculous levels of subservience and loyalty.

While all these attitudes may have been very useful in feudal Japan, in today's customer-centred West, it will result in you having a small school. You will never build a successful school that can support you (and your family) with such limiting beliefs holding you back. If you are serious about building a profitable school that allows you to live the life you want, you need to embrace modern business thinking and practices.

These include the following business concepts:

- A customer-centred approach (the customer is king).
- Great customer service, led with a smile (no more Mr. Grumpy instructor).
- Systemisation, so everything runs smoothly with or without you.
- Modern marketing techniques (the days of sticking up a few posters to attract students are long gone).
- Innovation (coming up with new ways of doing things).

Let's look at each of these modern business practices in detail.

A CUSTOMER-CENTRED APPROACH

In the old days, businesses sold stuff that they wanted to sell (think about Henry Ford's famous statement that customers can have a Model T Car in any colour they want as long as it's black). In those days, customers didn't have any choice. They had to buy from the only supplier in the market.

Today that's all changed. In your local area there are probably a dozen martial arts schools who are competing for the same student you are. Add in local fitness gyms, leisure centres, personal trainers, and bootcamps, and you have a lot of competition.

If you treat your prospects like the instructors of old, you will have empty classes. The modern customer has choice and power, and they know it. If they don't like how you treat them, they will leave, go somewhere else, and slag you off on Facebook.

To build a successful business, it's necessary to treat the customer with respect and genuine appreciation. You need to make your students feel special, valued, and appreciated, or they will quit. Customer service (along with marketing) is probably the most important factor in running a successful school. If you treat people right and consistently deliver a positive experience, your classes will be rammed.

In the "good old days", here is how an instructor would treat a new student.

They would:

- Ignore them
- Intimidate them
- Barely speak to them
- Beast them

And then

- Beat them up

And that's why they only had ten students. True those ten students were total beasts, and that's fine if you only want ten students. But if you want or need 100 students, you have to treat them as the most important people you know.

This includes doing the following:

- Learning their names (yes, really).
- Being genuinely interested in their lives.
- Talking to them after class.
- Complimenting them when they do well.
- Helping them without having to be asked.
- Caring about them.
- Being patient and kind.

If you can't do these things consistently, you will be destined to having a small school of "psychos" forever. Of course, there needs to be a professional relationship between instructor and student, but that doesn't stop you from learning their names or asking them how their day went. As the Americans say:
No one cares how much you know, till they know how much you care.

CUSTOMER SERVICE

This obviously ties in with being customer centred. If you are customer centred and constantly thinking of how you can improve your customers experience, then your customer service is likely to be outstanding. I define customer service as serving your customers beyond their expectations. Let's take a look at some customer service issues in the martial arts industry and note the differences between old school and new school practices.

1. Student has missed a grading.

Old school: *"Tough luck kid, you should have turned up at your grading, now give me 50 push-ups on your knuckles."*

New school: *Ask them why they missed the grading, schedule a catch-up grading or private grading and offer to do a free 15-minute private to make sure they are up to speed on the syllabus.*

2. Student can't afford to pay fees for one month.

Old school: *"See you in a month then, loser."*

New school: *Try to find out why they couldn't afford training. Tell them they can pay you back in instalments, but let them keep training. Or, even let them off that month entirely (only do this once though or some people may try to take advantage).*

3. Student is having trouble with a particular move.

Old school: *"Practice more."*

New school: *"Here let me find a black belt to help you get that move down. I will also send you some video I have filmed on how to master that move. Let's check in next week to see how it's coming along."*

Do you appreciate the difference? One is very traditional and impersonal, and the other is relaxed, thoughtful, and kind. Which do you think will get you more students? Which takes more effort? The new school, of course, but it pays back ten times what it costs. Students will tell everyone they know about your amazing customer service; they will also go out of their way to help you when you need it, and everyone has a lot more fun. Remember the heart of martial arts is about service and protecting the weak. There is no better way to demonstrate this than by taking care of your own customers.

ANSWERING THE PHONE

On the customer service side, one of the best things I ever did was invest in using a call answering service. This means that, if I don't answer a call, it gets forwarded to this service, and they pick up for me. They then follow a script I have written for them that goes like this:

Answering service: *"Hi, Masters Academy, how can I help?"*

Caller responds to the question.

Answering service: *"That's great, all our instructors are busy right now teaching,* can I get one to call you back soon?"

Caller answers the question.

Answering service: *"Fantastic and your number is?"*

Caller responds with their number.

Answering service: *"And you are calling about?"*

Caller responds with the reason for the call.

Answering service: *"That's great an instructor will call you back within a couple of hours. Thank you. Bye."*

Now, you may be thinking, "I don't need an answering service, I answer all my calls." I bet you don't. You don't answer when you are asleep, when you are training, when you are teaching, when you are driving, when your kids are screaming, and a whole range of other times.

The problem with that is many people don't leave a message, and they also don't call back. They might have a list of martial art school numbers and will work through the list till they get hold of someone. If you don't answer, you lose a prospective customer to your competition.

Since I started using my call answering service, I have had a 100 per cent increase in enquires. That means beforehand I was losing loads of leads by not answering my phone. Right now, I use an excellent service called AllDay PA, which answers my calls if I don't pick up within five rings, takes all the details I mentioned earlier, and emails me all the information in five minutes. It's brilliant, and they have helped me add dozens of students to my school by picking up the phone when I can't. I highly recommend them.

SYSTEMS (Save Your Self Time Energy Money)

Systemisation begins by writing down everything that happens in your business. Right from putting your key in the door and turning on the lights to how you market and sign up a student. You do this by recording everything you do in your business over a period. You will be surprised by how much you do and how much is automatic, so you don't even think about it.

The whole goal of systemisation is to allow your business to run without you. If you have to be there to do and manage everything, then all you have is a job, not a business.

A business is something that can run without you and still stay profitable. The main problem of most small business owners is that they do everything themselves. This is a problem because there are only so many hours in a day and so much energy in the tank. Eventually, something starts to slip.

During a particularly stressful time in my life, I took my eye off the ball regarding students who had cancelled. Within three months, we had lost 77 students. That is awful, and it happened because I was trying to do everything myself, and I dropped one of the many balls I was juggling.

If you systemise everything (that is write out every event, action, and process in your business), you can train someone to do many of those jobs. This frees up time for you to manage the systems, monitor performance, think, and innovate. McDonalds restaurants, for example, are typically run by teenagers and a few older managers. If you have any experience with teenagers, you may wonder how this is possible. It works because of its systems. McDonalds has systems and procedures for EVERYTHNG. This means with a bit of time and training a group of spotty teens can run a million pound fast food outlet by themselves.

Here's my question: Can you train up a group of teens to run your business while you go on holiday? Only joking, but you get my point. Do you have an operations manual that details how to do everything required to run your business? If not, you are destined to run it yourself forever till you die or give up.

You will need systems for:

- People (all the various roles in your business)
- Processes (how things happen in your business)
- Procedures (the way you want things to happen in your business)

In my case, the first step was to write down everything I did during 72 hours in my business. You are then left with a list of a 100 or more things that get done in your business over three days. Divide this list into groups: people systems, process systems, and procedure systems. Once they are divided into their groups, start simplifying and logging each individual step. Write them down, refine, review, test, and start training your staff.

You will need to create systems for:

- Training staff (paid and voluntary)
- Opening up & closing
- Answering the phone
- Answering emails
- Meeting prospects
- Intro lessons
- Teaching classes
- Equipment sales
- Dealing with complaints
- Stock checks
- Cashing up
- Cleaning
- First aid
- And loads more

Once you have systemised, it's possible to train someone to do the jobs in your business that you don't want to do or are of low priority. As the owner of your own business, it's very important to concentrate on high return tasks and not get bogged down in the daily nitty-gritty of running your club. To illustrate this idea here is a little test – below is a list of some high and low return tasks for a business owner.

Write beside each what would be a high or low value task for a business owner.

1. Cleaning the toilets
2. Answering the phone
3. Marketing & promotion
4. Picking up equipment from suppliers
5. Planning
6. Teaching the white belt classes
7. Teaching the black belt team
8. Cleaning the mats
9. Training your team
10. Tidying up after classes

11. Researching new developments in your industry
12. Printing certificates
13. Reading and implementing from business books
14. Going on Facebook to check out your news feed
15. Handing out flyers on the street
16. Going on Facebook to market to your prospects and customers

As you can now appreciate, some of these tasks create more value to your business than others. Any task of low priority that someone else can do you should systemise (so it's done your way). Find the right individual to do it, train him or her, and then let the person get on with it. This should hopefully free up a lot of time for you to focus on the things that will make a massive difference.

When you systemise your business make sure that you do the following:

- Record everything you do.
- Break everything down into simple steps.
- Don't assume anything. Write everything down (for example, put key in lock and turn clockwise to open door).
- Test all the systems to see if they do what you want them to do.
- Make sure you review the systems regularly to see if they can be improved.
- Monitor the results you are getting with the staff.
- Modify if needed.

MODERN MARKETING PRACTICES

Old school martial arts marketing meant handing out a handful of flyers on a Saturday afternoon in town. Or, doing an occasional school demo when you felt like it. In the last 20 years, marketing for the martial arts industry has come on in leaps and bounds. In my experience, the top-marketing techniques used today (and in order of importance) are as follows:

1. A converting website
2. Referral schemes
3. A social media presence
4. Social events in your school

5. Movie tie-ins

A CONVERTING WEBSITE

Twenty years the internet didn't exist, so everyone found martial arts classes in the yellow pages, via a friend, or they happened across a flyer. Since the birth of the Internet, the majority of new students (who don't come via referrals) come through the Internet. The first thing most young people do to find some information is "Google it."

Let's say that they get a sudden urge to try some kickboxing. They may go on a social-sharing site like Facebook and ask their friends if they know of a school or they may go straight to Google. On Google they will typically search for something like "kickboxing classes in (their town)". Now, if you have a well-constructed website that ranks highly on Google, your school should pop up at the top of the first page.

If you don't have a website (or your website is rubbish, and you are on page three), you have just lost a customer.

Recently we did a survey at my school to see how our last 100 prospects found out about us – 60 per cent came from referrals, 39 per cent came from the Internet, and 1 per cent came from a flyer. If you don't have a converting website, you are losing out on nearly 40 per cent of your potential customers and possibly higher.

A converting website, by the way, is a website that converts a prospect into a customer. There are major differences between a converting website and a normal martial arts school website.

A REGULAR MARTIAL ARTS SCHOOL WEBSITE

This website usually has a weird name like White Elbow Kung Fu and has a lot of information about the style, the instructor, their lineage, and the techniques they teach. So, basically, it's all about the instructor's ego. Look how great I am, look what I've done, look at my amazing credentials, etc. The problem is new students are not interested in you at all. All they care about is themselves and what you can do for them. Here's what they think of your site:

White Elbow Kung Fu ... "Sounds weird to me."
The styles' history ... "Boring."
The instructor's credentials ... "Don't understand any of this."
The techniques ... "That sure looks confusing/dangerous."
Next! And off they go to find another website. They make this decision in a couple

of seconds. Now, let's contrast that with a converting martial arts website.

A CONVERTING WEBSITE

The name of the site is www.KickboxingManchester.com, for example. So, you include the name of your town and main style in the web address.

At the very top of the page is a banner with your special offer. Free trial, free T-shirt and free private lesson. Underneath that are only two buttons: Click here for adult classes and click here for children's classes.

Let's look at a typical reaction to this site.

Kickboxing Manchester ... "That's good I live in Manchester."
Special offer ... "Wow, cool free stuff, will have to check this place out."
Choice of two buttons ... "OK, I'm interested in adult classes so I click here. This is easy."

And so on. The button they click lands them on a sales page about that programme, which includes the benefits for them and how they get started by contacting you.

This type of website will convert a person browsing into a person who calls and comes to try out a free class. Can you see how the Internet has changed marketing for martial arts schools? You desperately need a website that is constructed well, is simple to navigate, and gets people to give you a call. If your website does anything else, you are wasting time, energy, and money.

To create such a website, you will probably need the services of a web designer who can build websites. You can do it yourself with software such as WordPress, but a novice's first attempt at web design usually looks amateurish. It's worth spending a couple of hundred pounds to get a professional-looking, well-optimised site built.

It creates the right impression and helps people feel confident that you know what you are doing.

The best way to find a designer is to get recommendations from people who you trust. Failing that, do lots of online research and ask designers for examples of sites they have created, and check them out. Don't spend a lot of money on your site. A simple four-page site is all you need.

On your website you will need the following:

- An irresistible offer

- Keyword rich sales copy
- A compelling guarantee
- A short promo video
- Student testimonials
- Opt-in box with a free widget
- Attractive pictures of your students

IRRESISTIBLE OFFER

Your irresistible offer should be the first thing a prospect sees when they land on your site. This is because you only have three seconds to grab their attention. If they get lost or can't find anything interesting, they click off. You have to make them an amazing offer straight away. Then they will bother to view the rest of your site.

KEYWORD RICH SALES COPY COMES NEXT

You need to explain the benefits of training to your prospects via your sales copy. Don't talk about your style, your system, and your experience. Talk about THEM. That's all they care about ... themselves. Tell them how they will feel after training, explain how much weight they will lose, how toned they will get, and how it will make them less stressed and more happy. It's all about them and how their lives will be better as a result of training with you.

You also need to use the keywords that people will type into a search engine to find you. If they type kickboxing classes in Milton Keynes, and you don't mention kickboxing or Milton Keynes anywhere on your site, then the search engine can't find your site. You need to have a keyword rich website to help your search engine ranking (you want to rank number one on the first page).

MONEY-BACK GUARANTEE.

Since most adults train in martial arts for fitness, we offer a 60-day money-back guarantee that says, "If you don't see and feel the benefits of training with us twice a week for 60 days, we will refund all your money, no questions asked." This makes a prospect feel safe knowing that if they don't see benefits, they can get their money back. We haven't been asked to pay anyone's money back yet!

PROMO VIDEO

People like to watch videos and clips online. A short two to three minute promo of what you do and the benefits of training may help persuade prospects to give you a chance. Make it fast, exciting, and full of happy people having fun training.

Don't have people sparring, looking exhausted, or doing anything too crazy – it puts novices off.

TESTIMONIALS

The next essential for your website is having written and video testimonials. These testimonials act as social proof to your prospects that you can do what you say you can do, and that it actually works. If you have 20 testimonials scattered across your site, complimenting your skills, classes, and customer service, then people are more inclined to believe what you are saying. Have a mix of written and video testimonials to suit different types of prospects. Some people prefer the written word, and others like to watch videos. Testimonials are very powerful, so you must use them on all your marketing material.

OPT-IN BOX & WIDGET

Every page should have an opt-in box on it, preferably, in the top right-hand corner. An opt-in box (which links to an email autoresponder) captures the names and email addresses of people interested in your classes. It's advisable to use a widget to motivate people to give their email addresses.

A widget can be any free gift, which has value such as a free report, video, or a PDF of training tips. It should also be of interest to a person searching for martial arts classes. A free report about how to choose a good martial arts school would be an excellent widget for example. Once you have the prospect's email address you can send them information and special offers to try to encourage them to come in for a trial.

ATTRACTIVE PICTURES

Try to use attractive pictures of people having fun whilst training. Include pictures of men, women, kids, and teens training. Try not to use pictures that depict violence.

Prospects are scared enough without viewing pictures of people getting kicked in the face. Fit-looking, smiling, happy people work best.

Once you have your website built and launched make sure that you register the domain with all the major search engines. By registering your domain name, it means search engines will be able to find your site. This is very important.

You need to register with the three big search engines:

- Google
- Yahoo
- Bing

These powerhouses own 97 per cent of the market share when it comes to searches in the UK, and they will help your site get ranked quickly.

REFERRALS

When a student tries your classes and joins your academy, they are at their peak of motivation and excitement. They are having fun, meeting new people, getting fit, and learning a martial art. This is also the exact time when they will tell their friends what an amazing place your school is. They will do this naturally if you let them, encourage them, and remind them to tell their friends/family. You prompt them by having a systematised referral system in place.

This is a process you have created to ask for and get referrals from happy students.

Many people will automatically tell their social circle if they've found something new that they think their friends will enjoy. But quite a few people need a mental nudge to get them going. Here are some simple ideas you can use immediately to get more referrals.

*A reduction in the joining fee in exchange for two names and numbers of friends who might also enjoy martial arts.
*An entry into a raffle for a cool prize (like an iPad) in exchange for a referral.
*A cash prize for the most referrals in a month.
*A lucky dip bag for people who have referred a friend.
*An equipment voucher for the person who referred a friend.
*A free week or month's training for the person who referred a friend.
*Post a thank you on Facebook to anyone who refers a friend.

Choose one of these that you think will work, publicise it before and after every class, and try it out for a couple of months. It won't do any harm and may get you a lot of extra members for a minimal outlay. Referred customers are the best customers because they have been sold on the benefits of your gym by their friends. All you need to do is demonstrate what they already believe, and they will sign up immediately. If you don't have a formalised referral system, you may be missing out on 60 per cent of your potential customers.

SOCIAL MEDIA PRESENCE

A lot of people use social media sites like YouTube, Facebook, and Google+ to find things out about new interests. They may ask their Internet friends or see a post or advert for your school online. If you have a strong social media presence, you will be easy to find and can market to these people. At this time, Facebook is still the biggest social-sharing platform, so it's worth getting a Facebook page for your school set up ASAP. This will allow your students to comment, discuss, and share information which makes your clubs online presence stronger.

At the same time, you can market on your page (but not too much) and tag people in photos, which means your photos will appear in their news-feed. This may get their friends curious about the martial arts and recruit you new members. Always include your business website in every post, so people can click through to your site for more information.

There are, of course, many other things you can do with social media, competitions, stories, shares, boost posts, paid adverts, etc. But the most important thing is to have a Facebook page and share insights, comments, information, and videos everyday with your fans. This will over a period of time build into a large community of people, who are interested to hear what you have to say and will value your insight. This will make you the local online expert in martial arts. Once you have done this on Facebook, it is a good idea to do the same on other social media sites like Google + and Pinterest. The more social media you can do, the bigger your sphere of influence. You will be amazed at the opportunities that will come your way through social media.

IN-SCHOOL SOCIAL EVENTS

We do a lot of in-school social events. Going to watch fights, picnics, parties, post grading celebrations, among others, all help build the strong "family" feeling we want to encourage. But you can also do external events to get more clients. Events like a "Bring a Buddy Day," where kids bring a non-martial arts friend with them to class work well. Teach a really fun class and give each kid a free two-week pass, a T-shirt and many will come back to sign up.

Or, you could try a "parent and kids" class where the parents get to help teach their kids. This involves them in their kids' activities. Some parents enjoy it so much that they start training as well. How about having a demonstration. Find a local event, offer to do a demonstration, and get ten of your top students to put on a great demo. It builds team spirit and attracts new students. Or an open day, where you invite the student's friends and family to come look around the school, and try out a few ten-minute taster sessions.

MEDIA TIE-INS

You know the Kung Fu Panda movie right? Even if you don't have kids, you know what he looks like. What we did is order a replica Kung Fu Panda suit from China, and, every weekend during the summer, we walk up and down our high street, handing out kickboxing flyers to kids. You should see the kids' faces when they see Kung Fu Panda walking down the street. They literally run towards him, dragging their parents with them. We give them a flyer and tell them about the benefits of martial arts. They usually take a photo with the panda, and we get a lot of calls the next week. It works like a charm and has done well for us for the three years we have had the panda suit. As long as they keep releasing Kung Fu Panda films, we will keep walking about in our suit.

When London held the Olympics, we were interviewed by the local newspaper about how it affected our business. They did a full-page interview for free, and it helped us get a lot of local exposure. You need to take full advantage of any regional or local media events that could boost your business. Unfortunately, we live in a celebrity-obsessed world right now, so anything that is popular and well known (like the Kung Fu Panda) will help sell your school. Some martial arts instructors have even got into fight choreography for movies (like Batman) and use the hype around Batman to sell their martial arts programmes.

If you do each of these five key marketing activities every week, you will attract lots of fresh leads. You can still do the traditional marketing techniques, such as flyer drops and poster hanging, but be aware that they may not be very targeted or effective. Leaflet drops commonly have a success rate of less than one per cent meaning that ninety-nine per cent of your leaflets go into the bin. But, of course, if you have a compelling offer, a good headline, and a strong call to action, you may do better off leafleting. Test it and find out.

TEST

You need to test everything you do with your marketing to see if it's working. If you do a 10,000 leaflet drop and it costs you £400, you need to know how many people join as a result of this tactic. If only one person joins, then it costs you £400 to buy that client. That's pretty expensive! Perhaps, you might try a different headline next time or drop leafleting altogether, and try something a little more targeted. Buying a panda outfit from China cost us £150 and each time we take it out, we get five calls minimum and three kids usually join our school. This means it has paid for itself numerous times over the past three years.

It's also very targeted. Kids and parents come rushing over to see it, so we know exactly who we will attract. The five marketing ideas we mentioned: website conversion, referrals, social media, social events, and media tie-ins don't cost a lot when compared with traditional marketing activities. For example, I have a school-owner friend who spent over £5000 on a radio advert that played out for a few weeks in his town and brought in ZERO students. Traditional media marketing (paper, print, radio, TV) is slowly becoming less effective. The rules have changed, and you need to get with the times.

MARKETING MINIMUMS

You know what it's like – one month you're on top of your marketing and its going well. Then something happens in your personal life or you just get lazy and boom! You notice that you are not getting as many enquires and your classes are a little quieter. So, you get back to marketing. This up and down method of marketing is stressful, time consuming, and leads to inconsistent growth.

As with martial arts training, marketing needs to be consistent to work effectively. This is mainly because people need to see your marketing repeatedly before they act. Ad experts believe that a prospect will need to see your ad (online or offline) six or seven times before they choose to take action.
If your flyer is delivered once to 5000 houses and not delivered again in three months you won't make an impression. If you are going to do flyer drops, you will need to set up a campaign where you hit the same houses repeatedly over a three- to six-month period.

Why? Well this is how flyering works:

1. Person gets flyer at door advertising martial arts.
2. They glance at it briefly and throw it in the bin.
3. Person gets second flyer.
4. They think "kickboxing … nah, not for me," and throw it in the bin.
5. Person gets third flyer.
6. They read it and think, "Well, maybe, I should do some exercise," then they throw it in the bin.
7. Person gets the fourth flyer.
8. They think, "Hmmm, maybe, I should give these guys a call, but not now," and they put the flyer in a drawer.
9. Person gets the fifth flyer.
10. "Oh, yeah, I was going to call them, I will do it tonight," and then they don't.
11. Person gets sixth flyer.
12. "Right, I need to get in shape, so I will call them now."

You get a call (and if you don't answer, you've wasted all that marketing). This is why a call answering service is vital.

As you can now surmise, doing a single flyer drop is very inefficient. You need a sustained assault to make flyers work, which means spending a lot of money. Conversely, if you advertise online or on social media, you can knock together a new advert in seconds and post it for free. The same rules apply, as people will need to see your online ad several times before they respond, but online it doesn't cost you anything. There are no printing costs and no delivery charges you just post it up and it's done. As a start-up, it's vital to minimize your expenses, so any marketing you can do cheaply or for free needs to be used before you start spending on primetime

TV adverts after Coronation Street (only joking).

At my school, we have our marketing minimums, which we do every month come rain or shine, hail or snow. These are the MINIMUM marketing activities we perform every month to keep a steady stream of emails and calls coming in.

1. New offer on website

We change our offer regularly to see if it out performs our control advert. Our control is the best converting ad we have created so far. We try changing the headline, the offer, the font, the colour, and see if it works better than our control. If it does, then that's our new control advert. Currently, our most successful offer that gets us the most enquires is this one:

"Free Trial, Free T-shirt & Free Fitness Test"

2. Referral scheme

We try different referral schemes every two months. This keeps students on their toes and generates a little excitement – "What! This month we can win an iPad if we refer someone, awesome." Keep trying new referral systems and see what works best for you.

3. Social media adverts

The important thing with social media posts is to add value or make someone laugh. Adding value means posting something useful, such as "10 Self-defence tips for teens," "How to lose belly fat," "5 tips to improve your flexibility."

By sharing something that will improve your fans lives, you generate goodwill. Then once in a while you can advertise a new course or new class, and people will be more receptive and likely to share. Try to post tips daily, and make a special offer once a week.

A lot of businesses are using pay per click (PPC) advertising now, whether on Google, Facebook, or other sites. While this seems tempting, you really need to know what you are doing with regards to keyword selection, copy writing, and split testing. If all these terms are unfamiliar to you, DON'T do PPC advertising till you have read up on how to do it correctly. I didn't know initially what I was doing, so I lost £500 on useless ads. It was totally my fault, and I now have learnt how to use PPC advertising correctly. There are a number of good books and online courses about how to use PPC, so get educated first. You have been warned.

4. Social events at your school

Run some of these sessions on a regular basis:

Parent training sessions
Kids' Birthday parties (where they invite their non-martial arts friends)
Open days (where local people can come and check out your school)
Press releases on events (gradings, competitions, events, seminars)
Charity fundraising
Picnics
Parties
Seminars
Free workshops for local kids
Self-defence talks
These events will get people talking, coming in, and getting interested in what you do.

5. Movie tie-ins

Is there a new Karate Kid, TMNT, MMA, Ong Bak, Raid, Kung Fu Panda film coming out? Do an event or hire a costume and get out in your town handing out flyers. I started martial arts 28 years ago off Bruce Lee's Enter the Dragon. Movies work by getting people excited about martial arts. Make sure you use the buzz they create.

6. Posters & flyers

While I'm not a massive fan of random flyer drops, they do have their place. The main thing is that they need to be more targeted. So, we put out 1000–3000 flyers every month in specific places where our customers are likely to be found.

We put 50 or so in these locations:

- Local sports shops
- Local health food stores
- Local gyms (if they let us)

- Hair Salons
- Supermarket notice boards
- News agents' windows
- Tanning salons
- Kids' sweet shops

These places are where my target market are most of the time, so it makes sense to leave flyers for them to pick up. .

7. Joint ventures

Joint ventures, in this instance, refers to getting other local businesses to refer their customers to you and vice versa. Basically, you go and speak to the person in charge, and ask them if they would be interested in referring their customers to you if you will do the same for them. You then swap business cards and, when anyone mentions that they need a physiotherapist, you whip out their card and recommend them. They will do the same for you when a customer mentions wanting to get fit.

Here is a list of possible businesses that may be willing to do a JV with a martial arts school:

Physiotherapists
Chiropractors
Osteopaths
Personal trainers
Sports injury specialists
Toy shops
Health food stores
Sports shops
Cafes
Gyms

All it takes to set this up is the time to go and ask each business owner about the possibility of doing a JV. It doesn't cost you anything to ask, and you can get yourself a few extra students a month from these joint ventures.

These are the minimum marketing you should be doing each and every month, and during your early days you should probably be doing twice as much.

SWOT ANALYSIS

SWOT stands for Strengths, Weaknesses, Opportunities, and Threats. This method of analysing your business has been around a long time, but it is still a useful tool to use when marketing.

STRENGTHS

What are you school's strengths? Customer service, attention to detail, fitness, fighting pedigree. What are you good at and what makes your club special? What you discover here should be the main thrust of your marketing message. For example, if your strengths are that you create great fighters, then you need to market to people who want to be fighters.

WEAKNESSES

What are your business weaknesses? Common weaknesses include inconsistent untested marketing, poor communication with students, problems tracking payments, and a lack of systematisation. You cannot fix a problem you are unaware of.

You need to know you have a problem before you can do anything about it, so get honest and analyse where you are weak. Then take the necessary steps to fix any weaknesses.

OPPORTUNITIES

What opportunities can you see approaching on the horizon? New premises, new classes, new location, improved lesson planning, assistant instructor training. Here you can get creative and think up as many opportunities as you can, and then work through them to find the gems that will make the biggest difference.

THREATS

What threatens your business right now? For me, it's usually my own ignorance and stubbornness that is the greatest threat to my business. Frequently, I am totally unaware of things that could have a massive effect on my business. Take music licensing, for example. For years I didn't know it existed. It wasn't until another instructor told me that I needed it, and that there was a £3000 fine if I didn't have a licence. Only then did I become aware of its seriousness.

That's why being a member of a professional body like the Federation of Small Businesses (FSB) is really useful. The FSB keep you aware of any changes to legislation that may affect you. Other threats may be greedy landlords, disloyal instructors, and other martial arts schools opening in your area.

COMPETITION ANALYSIS

Speaking of competitors, it's always worthwhile considering what your competition is doing in your local area. This will allow you to adjust your marketing to differentiate yourself from other martial arts schools. If you are the same as all the other martial arts schools in your area in the way you advertise or promote your school, then the customer can only compare you based on price. That's because you all look the same to them. However, if you have something unique and special about your school then you can differentiate yourself and dominate the market.

Some classic differences you can highlight include these points:

- Full-time school vs. Local part-time schools
- Full-time studio vs. Church hall classes
- Your type of client vs. Everybody else's clients
- New equipment you have vs. No equipment elsewhere
- Your parking facilities vs. Parking in a pay and display car park

All these differences can be emphasised in your marketing to position your school as superior to the local competition. If you appear superior to your prospects, half the battle is won. Try to find the unique thing that makes you different from your competitors, and highlight it on your website, social media, and flyers.

Of course, if your competitor seems to have all the advantages, you will need to do some work turning your weaknesses into strengths. For example a full-time school will generally have higher costs and will have to charge more, whereas a church hall operation can charge less and still remain competitive. Or, if the larger school specializes in training adults, you can focus you energy on dominating the kids' market in your local area. You will need to think creatively, but it is possible to go up against bigger competition and win, – and isn't that the whole idea of martial arts anyway?

LIFETIME STUDENT VALUE

This is an important concept because it should influence how you treat your prospects and students. I have walked into schools where the instructor is training as I enter. They often don't stop what they are doing and barely even recognise my presence – instant lost customer. Martial arts instructors are often guilty of thinking they haven't lost any money if a person doesn't sign up. This is not accurate, because they have already lost the cost of their advertising to get the student through the door. Once the student is there, you need to understand the lifetime value of that person to your business. Let's say your average student stays with you for eight months (hopefully longer, but it's just an example).

During that eight months, our students typically spend:

Training fees = £320
Joining fees = £60
Gradings = £80
Equipment purchases = £100
Seminars = £50
Private lessons (one a fortnight at £40) = £640

Total = £1250

Using this example, each new student that walks through the door is worth over £1000 to your business. If you ignore them, belittle them, leave them hanging, you are possibly throwing away a grand each time. Shame on you!

Nothing you are doing at that time is worth £1000, so drop whoever you are choking, excuse yourself, and go talk to the prospect. Be warm, be welcoming. They should feel like they are visiting an old friend. In bigger schools, this would be the job of a receptionist, but assuming you are on your own, it's down to you to make a great first impression. If you have assistants, they could deal with this, but it's such a vital moment that you would need to train them extensively on how to meet and greet new clients correctly. Generally, I like to do it if I can.

MONEY

As we are speaking about lifetime value, this seems like a good time to start discussing money. If you are opening or running a school that will take payments in exchange for tuition, you are running a commercial club. And if you are running a commercial club, you will want it to be as profitable as possible.

I guess most of you will still be working your day jobs as you set up your club in the evenings. This means you will be sacrificing your free time (time to relax, spend with the family, etc.) to run your club a couple of evenings a week. You should get paid well for this time. Taking home £25 after teaching three classes in one night sucks. You bust your ass, extend yourself, and teach your heart out and, while your students may be happy, you have got paid just over £8 an hour. Not great seeing as you have invested hundreds of hours and thousands of pounds in your own training. You need to start seeing yourself as a professional and start being paid as a professional. A lawyer, for example, will spend a decade getting qualified and will charge £200+ an hour for his or her services. You have also spent a decade or more in your training.

Do you think your expertise in your chosen art is worth £200 an hour? Well, I think my time is, and I'm constantly working to get paid that. In my journey to being a school owner, I have spent a ton of money on my martial arts education. Including:

- Training six different martial arts to black belt level and beyond.

- Testing my skills and courage fighting in the cage.
- Completed a university degree in Sports Science that left me ten grand in debt.
- Paid for and completed a sport's nutrition course.
- Paid for and completed a gym instructor's course.
- Signed up for numerous expensive online courses to do with running a martial arts business.
- Spent days away from home at workshops on Internet advertising, Facebook,
- Adwords, Twitter, etc.
- Read three books a week on areas of interest to me to do with martial arts.
- Bought 100s of DVDs on training and business.

All this experience has value – a lot of value if you market it well.

So let's go back to our class that you teach in the evenings after work. You are going to teach it anyway and get paid peanuts, so you might as well fill it and earn £200 a night or more. Plus, it's also easier to teach a bigger class in my opinion, as the energy from the group builds me up.

You need to value your expertise and realise how much you contribute to people's lives. Teaching Martial arts is not like curing cancer or anything that amazing, but it has a massive impact in many people's lives. Over the years, I have had students and parents tell me about the many positive side effects of martial arts, which include the following:

1. Losing weight
2. Being able to defend themselves
3. Getting fit
4. Winning titles
5. Leaving abusive partners
6. Handling bullies confidently
7. Managing their stress
8. Confidence in other areas of their lives
9. Improving body image
10. Controlling fear in tense situations
11. Giving them a purpose in life
12. Calming them down

13. Making them happy

14. Meeting like minded people

Martial arts is important in our student's lives, and there is nothing wrong with getting financially rewarded for the positivity we create.

So, if you are still only charging £3 a class, start to value yourself and what you do. Be proud of what you do, so you can charge what you are truly worth.

FINANCIALLY, WHERE ARE YOU AT NOW?

In business, you are either in one of three financial states: making a loss, breaking even, or making a profit. Obviously, making a loss is to be avoided at all costs, because eventually you will run out of money and enthusiasm, and close down. This happens when your expenses are more than your income.

Getting to break even is better, but it doesn't allow for any growth or investment in your business. In profit is where you want to be. Profit is where all the fun is. You can build your business, hire staff, save, or invest your profits, or even take a cheeky holiday. You want to be "in profit" as soon as possible.

In the early days of your business, all profits should be reinvested back into your business. Once you have paid all your expenses, any money left should be used to market, purchase equipment if needed, or improve your business education. Let's say you have £10 left as profit after your class. The temptation is to spend it on a pint or lottery tickets or other trivial item.

A better use for your £10 profit might be to buy a book on martial arts marketing. That way you're investing in yourself and building you knowledge. If you have £500 profit after your expenses are paid, it might be tempting to buy a new laptop. While this might be useful for your business, there are better uses for such a sum of money.

Profit in my business is funnelled into the following activities (and in order of importance in my opinion).

1. Paying tax in advance.

2. Building an emergency fund (3–6 months money needed to keep you going

if you suddenly lose all your students or your business premises burn down).

3. Tested marketing (marketing that is guaranteed to get results).

4. Invested in technology to improve my business.
5. Invested in training to improve my business.
6. Spent on improving the look of my academy

That's my personal order of priority. Yours may be different. Personally, I prefer not to have the tax man chase me for money I owe. I sleep better at night knowing it's all been paid in advance. I don't like being a fugitive from the law.

Next, I like to have an emergency fund for my business and personal life. If the shit hits the fan, and you can't work or need five grand for a new boiler, it's very reassuring to know you have it saved. I think you should have two emergency funds. One for your business, and one for you personally. Set up a standing order to a savings account that you don't touch and let it build. Do not touch this money unless it is needed for a genuine emergency.

Once I have paid my tax and got enough in my emergency fund, I then like to use profits for extra marketing. I, of course, have a monthly marketing budget, but sometimes an extra cash injection can help push you to the next level. But you shouldn't use this money on untested random marketing. Chucking £500 at AdWords without knowing what you are doing will probably lose you £500 in a couple of weeks. If you know what marketing works for you, then do more of it and keep an eye on your results.

Technology as we all know can help or hinder. As your school grows from 20 to 150 students, you will naturally start to lose track of things. There is only so much you can remember or write down on pieces of paper. Investing in good school management software will help you keep an eye on all the balls up in the air. Software will enable you to track your marketing, prospect calls, intro lessons, new members, birthdays, student details, grades, attendance, retention rates, and lots more. This is part of systematising your school, and, once you know how to use the software, it allows you to get an accurate picture of what's happening in your school at a click of a mouse. Another advantage of using a tuition billing company such as NEST management is that you get to use their martial arts school software for free, and they will train you on how to use it.

On the self-education front, you can use profits for your own martial arts or business training. From the business education standpoint, there are a number of options. You can buy books, DVDs, online training programs, attend workshops, go to seminars, or pay for a consultant. It's probably best to start small and read around your area of interest first. Buy some DVDs or an online program and spend more as you go. Unfortunately, in the martial arts business, there are a few shady characters around, who will happily take five grand off you and teach you rehashed material or dodgy business practices. Try not to fall under their spell when they tell you the stories of clubs growing by 100 students in a month. They are usually con men who sell get-rich-quick schemes and make their living off the gullible. If your intuition tells you it's too good to be true, it usually is. Always research anyone you are taking advice from to see if they are telling the truth. At some point you may consider using a business coach as they can give you an external view of your business and more importantly cut through the bullshit and keep you honest.

UPDATING THE ACADEMY

Equipment gets damaged or worn out, and so it needs to be replaced regularly. If equipment is left in a poor state, it leads to increased risk of injury, infection, and creates a really funky smelling school. A great idea when it comes to replacing any piece of kit, whether it be a bag glove or a punch bag, is not to wait till it's virtually destroyed before replacing. Instead, as soon as any bit of club kit looks at bit worn, put it in your pro shop and sell it as used kit.

Students can then buy it at a discount, and you can use the money to buy new kit at trade price. That way your club always has new shiny kit, and students can purchase part worn kit (but still good) cheaply. I used to think this wouldn't work, who would want a second-hand pair of focus mitts after all? But when I actually tried it, the students loved it. They got a pretty decent pair of used mitts for half the regular price. What's not to love?

You can also use profits to upgrade the look of your academy. A fresh coat of paint, new toilets and boosting lighting can have a massive effect on how professional you school looks to prospects.

Of course, you don't need to do this, and, when I started out, I often spent any profit on tasty meals out, trinkets, and gadgets. But as I started to get wiser, I realised that I was wasting money on stuff I didn't want or need, and that the money would be better used reinvested back into my business to build future profits.

HOW TO GET MORE PROFIT

There is a common saying in business that "turnover is vanity and profit is sanity." What's the point in having a £250,000 turnover if your expenses are £251,000? What really matters in business is how much profit you make. Profits allow you to save, invest, expand, hire staff, or take a holiday. Everything gets a lot easier if you consistently make a profit year on year and manage that profit wisely.

Profit happens as a result of turnover exceeding expenses. As long you earn more than you spend, you will be making a profit. Expenses in business include:

- Rent
- Rates
- Utilities

- Staff payroll
- Marketing
- Equipment depreciation
- Insurance
- Saving for tax

A general principle of business is to keep your expenses as low as possible. When renting, for example, you could lease a 5,000 sq. ft. unit, and kit it out with all the latest stuff, but if you only have 50 students and their combined income doesn't pay your bills, you would be in trouble pretty quickly. In the early stages, you want your expenses to be as low as possible to enable you to grow quickly and sustainably.

THE COSTS OF DOING BUSINESS

RENT

Jumping straight into owning a full-time gym without a stable customer base, startup capital, or marketing is extremely dangerous. Most martial arts schools operate out of church halls for a reason. They are cheap and usually large. This means you will only need a handful of students to cover the rent. Try to find cheap spaces to rent in a good location, with plenty of parking, and try not to pay too much for them.

Negotiate a rent-free period while you set up your class or get a reduction if you pay in advance for a period. Most church/sports hall managers are willing to help you out if you ask politely.

RATES

Rates will only apply if you take on a business unit. You are then usually responsible for paying the local council for the rates. There is no room for negotiation here so make sure you are fully aware of the rates you will have to pay before you sign the lease. You may however be eligible for small business rates relief, so do some research before you sign anything.

UTILITIES

Once again, only really applicable if you are taking on a full-time space. Utilities include gas, electricity, phone line, etc. You will have to factor in how much these utilities will cost you and when they need to be paid. Paying by direct debit is probably best as it automates the payment and stops you forgetting to pay and having your electricity cut off. Ask your landlord or neighbours how much they anticipate these bills will be. You could also consider changing utility supplier if there is a better deal elsewhere.

PAYROLL

If you are just starting out, you will likely be the only staff member. So the question becomes whether you pay yourself or leave the money in the business. If you don't need the money to survive, it's probably best to leave it in the business where it can be used more effectively. Once you start growing at some point, you will need help teaching, otherwise, you risk burnout. This help can either be voluntary or paid.

Both have their problems from a legal and tax perspective. It is vital to speak to a specialist martial arts business accountant, such as Dennis and Turnbull about this minefield before you start hiring help.

MARKETING COSTS

These are the costs of getting students in and paying via advertising. It is preferable to keep these as low as possible in the start. A lot of marketing can be done without spending any or little money. Referrals, demos, talks, VIP passes, press releases, and social media don't cost a lot of money, but they do require time. But at the start, you will probably have plenty of time and not much money, so get to it. Dedicate an hour a day (minimum) to low-cost marketing for your school.

Even getting a four-page website built is pretty cheap these days. As you grow, your marketing costs will tend to grow as well.

INSURANCE

You will need several types of insurance to run your martial arts school safely. First of all, you will need public liability insurance which covers the cost of legal action and compensation claims made against you if a third party is injured whilst at your business premises. So if a parent slips and injures their knee whilst at your school and decides to sue, you are covered (hopefully ... as we all know what insurance companies are like).

The second type of insurance you will need is public indemnity insurance. This is a type of coverage designed to protect an individual or a business against claims made by clients due to negligent advice or service. So, if you do something or make a mistake and a student gets injured and decides to sue, you should be protected (with the same warning as before). The most important thing to do is find insurance companies that deal with martial arts specifically, as they will understand the industry better. Secondly, make sure you get the maximum coverage you can afford.

Read all their information they supply regarding your coverage and their requirements, and follow their guidelines to the letter, documenting everything as you go.

EQUIPMENT DEPRECIATION

Martial arts equipment gets broken quickly. Gloves, pads, shields, bags, and mats all need replacing yearly (at least). This costs money, especially the mats, so you need to factor in how much depreciation will cost you throughout the year.

TAX

As a martial arts instructor you are likely to be self-employed or part of a partnership.

You therefore need to plan how you will pay your National Insurance (NI) and tax. In order to pay your tax on time and in full, you will need to know how much you have to save each month to pay your bill in January and July. This is a job for a good bookkeeper or accountant. You can do this yourself, but, unless you enjoy it, you won't do it, and it will pile up until you have a total mess on your hands.

Pay a bookkeeper to do your books once a month or once a quarter. Then they will be able to tell you how much to save each month to cover your tax bill in January and July.

Or you can set up a direct debit with the Inland Revenue and pay your tax off in advance, which is what I prefer to do. I would rather be ahead and overpaying a little than behind, because the HMRC will start fining you once you are 30 days late. Go to the HMRC website and search paying your tax with direct debit. You can set up a DD to go out of your account the day after you get paid each month, and you won't even miss the money. Then when your bill comes round in January, you will have paid off most, if not all of it. That's a very nice feeling believe me.

When I first started out, I didn't do this and when my bill would turn up in January I would have to find £10,000 or more within 30 days to avoid a fine. Stupid. Eventually, I got smarter and starting paying my tax off in advance via DD, and for some years when I got my bill, I was actually in credit. Happy.

MISC. EXPENSES

There may be other expenses that occasionally crop up such as travel expenses, printing expenses, or office materials. For the moment we will group them as miscellaneous expenses. In most martial arts schools, the rent and rates, staff payroll, utilities, and equipment purchases will be the major expenses.

Once you have added up all your expenses and made provision for repairs and unexpected catastrophes, you will be able to calculate your expenses for the month.

BREAK EVEN

The break-even point for your business is where income is equal to expenses. After the break-even point, any extra income will be profit as long as your costs stay the same. You need to know your break-even point in advance. The goal is to get to break even as soon as possible, and then start making profit. You calculate your break-even point by working out your fixed costs plus your variable costs each month.

Fixed costs are stable each month, such as rent, payroll, and insurance, plus saving for taxes and your marketing budget.

Variable costs can change each month. Utility bills, travel, repairs, cleaning, and office supplies can all change from month to month.
If you calculate your fixed costs and add your variable costs, you have your break-even point. Once you earn this amount, all your expenses can be paid, but you are not yet in profit.

One fixed costs I haven't included are loan repayments. If you're just starting out from a rented hall, you probably won't need a loan as your start-up costs should be pretty low. But if you taking on leased premises, you may need extra capital to cover redecorating, buying mats, pads, gloves, bags, mirrors, reception desk, computer, stationary, pro shop supplies, etc. This all adds up and before you know it, you calculate that you will need £10,000 to open. That's OK if you have the money yourself, but, if you don't, you will need funding from somewhere. Many people ask their families first. This can be risky, and there is the potential to really screw things up. You need to think very hard before taking money from your family:

- What happens if it doesn't work out?
- When will you repay the money?
- How will you repay the money?
- Will any interest be charged?
- If you lose their money, will they ever speak to you again?
- Is it worth the stress?

Only you can answer these questions, but from personal experience, I have borrowed small sums of money from my family when the business needed it. But when it needed a big cash injection, I went straight to my bank. I have had several loans from my bank over the years, and, as long as you are aware that they will come for the money if you default, they are a reliable source of money when it's needed.

Generally, to lower your risk when starting up, it's best to not take out any loans until you are well into sustainable profits. Do everything yourself, grow gradually, source cheap supplies, and penny pinch wherever possible. It's not very exciting or glamorous, but it's safer and more manageable.

Once you know your break-even point, you can formulate a plan to reach it as soon as possible. You do this by calculating your break-even point, and then working out how much your average student spends with you each month (including class fees, joining fees, equipment purchases, seminars, private lessons, etc.). You can then work out how many students you will need to reach your break-even point.

Be aware that you will have to factor in attrition, which is the rate that you lose students each month. Every martial arts school in the world loses a certain percentage of their students each month to injury, illness, moving away, job changes, money problems, and boredom. You can, of course, do many things to reduce your attrition, and we will look at this later in the book.

THE CHAPTER YOU HAVE BEEN WAITING FOR

HOW TO MAKE MORE MONEY

Jay Abraham, the marketing genius, is fond of saying that there are only three ways to build your business:

1. Acquire more customers.
2. Increase the size of the average purchase.
3. Increase the frequency of purchase.

That's it. I like simplicity, so that's how I try to increase my income.

1. ACQUIRE MORE CUSTOMERS

This is, in Jay's opinion, the hardest way to grow your business as you have to get new clients, which can be expensive and time consuming. We have already covered some ideas on how to market your business with the marketing minimums. If you want more customers, you are going to have to do more effective marketing. That means either doing more of what you are currently doing or trying something new to see if it works better.

Dan Kennedy the marketing expert once said:

> *I don't know 1 way to get 100 new customers, but I do know 100 ways to get 1 customer.*

Obviously, you need to be focusing on the main ways to get customers, which for us would be via referral and our website. But you also want to be doing 10, 20, or 50 other marketing activities every month to bring in extra customers from other sources. The Internet is an amazing tool for informing and selling to customers, but, unless they are actively looking for your site, they won't stumble across it accidentally.

However, if you have advertised in a local newsagent's window, then people on the street may come across your advert accidentally. They will also walk past it for weeks, as a result it will keep prompting them to think about giving your school a try. So while you have your marketing major players, you will also want to investigate using other low tech methods to build your business.

These include the ones discussed in the marketing minimums and the following:

Local paper advertising

Don't be tempted to do a single massive ad in your local paper. A better idea is to contact your paper's advertising editor a day or two before it goes to press and offer to put a small ad in for a reduced price. Frequently, they need a space to be filled and say yes. You can then offer to do a series of small ads for 3–6 months at a discount.

With newspaper advertising, you need to understand that a prospect will have to see your ad repeatedly before they act. Make sure the ad has a benefit-oriented headline. For example, "Lose Weight Fast with Kickboxing" is better than "New Kickboxing Class." The first headline gives a clear benefit "you will lose weight fast," which is much more appealing. And please make sure your ad has a call to action. Don't just write about your school and end with your phone number, instead try something like "Call now for your free trial, limited spaces available." This invites them to call and also makes the offer urgent, because there are only a finite number of spaces.

Coupon sites

Right now coupon sites like Wowcher and Groupon are very popular. How long that lasts is up for debate, but you can use them for a very specific purpose. Let's say you have a class on a Friday night that is dead. You only get five or six students attending each week, and you are thinking of closing it. You could put an advert on Wowcher, for example, for 10 kickboxing classes for £25. Now that is a ridiculously low rate, and it would be a disaster if you allowed people to pay that little for classes in peak times. But, in our Friday night class, it might work well to fill it up, get people used to coming in and earning a little extra money.

With all voucher sites, you can stipulate where and what the voucher is for. So you simply put in the description:

Voucher only valid for classes on Friday evenings.

Bingo you have filled your Friday class and, once the voucher expires, you can upgrade the students to your regular class or offer them a deal on Friday night training only. The only problem we have encountered with customers that come from voucher sites is that they tend to be very price conscious, so they may not stick around after the deal is up. But, if you don't try, you never know.

Local magazines

If you like writing, it is possible to offer your services to local magazines as their "health & fitness expert." Then once a month you write an article on a particular fitness subject and include a link to your website at the bottom of the page. That way you position yourself as an expert in your local community, and you get to advertise your school for free.

School drops

This is a big one if you teach kid's classes. You phone up a school and ask to deliver some flyers to them. If they accept, which they will if you are nice and charming, you batch them in groups of 30 and hand them in to the school. The school will then distribute them to the kids for you. Amazing. Once again make sure you have a compelling headline, a great picture of kids' training, an irresistible offer, and a call to action.

Flyering on the street

This is what it says – standing on the street handing out flyers. This is probably not the best use of your time, but a student may be interested in doing it in exchange for some free lessons or cash. The good thing about this method of advertising is that you can pick and choose who to give the flyer to. The 80-year-old lady may not be interested in your kickboxing class, but the 25-year-old woman probably will be.

If the flyers you are going to hand out are for a specific group, this makes it easier for you. If you have kids' kickboxing flyers, then obviously target families walking by.

And make sure the flyer has a compelling headline etc. It also helps to have an attractive person handing out the flyer, because more people are more likely to notice them and engage. Sad but true.

Yellow pages / Thompson local

The days of the paper yellow pages are limited, but, as long as they offer a free listing, what harm can it do. I don't know anyone who uses these directories anymore, but there must be some people who do. So put in a simple, irresistible offer and see what you get.

Poster boards

Get a big poster printed onto a wooden billboard and pay a student to hold it near a major road, close to your academy during rush hour. Make it brightly coloured, so it catches the eye, and make the text large, bold, and easy to read. A simple message will work, such as the following:

FREE KICKBOXING CLASSES HERE

People will then stop and speak to the student holding the sign, and they can direct them in or give them a flyer if appropriate. Once again an attractive person works best.

Building signs

Unfortunately, we are not allowed to advertise on the outside of our building, but if you can advertise, get the biggest and brightest sign that you can afford. You wouldn't believe how blind people are. They can stand next to your school and still not see it. So make your sign bright, MASSIVE, interesting, and include an offer.

Business cards

I'm still amazed by the number of martial arts instructors who don't have business cards. They are free on many sites. Get 250 done and make sure you include an offer and a call to action on the back. I get asked for my contact details at least once a week, so it's worth doing and makes you appear more professional than writing your number on a scrap of paper.

Car decals

If you have a nice car, you could use it to advertise your school. Several of my students have done this with their schools and have got calls from people who have seen their cars. Don't do this if you have a beaten-up car, it just gives the wrong impression. But if you have a nice car or van and you don't mind it, you can turn your vehicle into a 24/7 portable advertising machine.

Car window stickers

Do a bit of research and get some window stickers made for your students' cars. Your students live and drive in your local area, so help them advertise for you. Get 100 cool-looking back-window stickers made and give them to your students for free.

Signs in your windows

You need to let people look into your school before they step inside. Blacked-out windows are off-putting as people don't know what they are getting into. But you can also do some marketing with posters and signs in your windows to get people to come inside. The following is good:

Come in and have a chat to see how we can help you lose weight, burn fat, and have fun whilst learning a kick-ass martial art.

By the way, don't write this on a piece of paper in biro. Print it, frame it and make it look professional, please.

2. INCREASE THE AVERAGE SIZE OF A PURCHASE BY A STUDENT.

This is easier to do as your students already know you, like you, and trust you. Therefore they are interested in what you have to say and your recommendations. In a martial arts context, you could consider two different options here.

First, you can provide a wider range of classes for your students to upgrade to. With this option, you tier your classes from fundamental classes right through to black belt clubs. As the students go up the levels, the price increases. But with every price increase, you need to add twice as much value so the student is happy.

This is commonly done by lengthening the length of the sessions, adding extra dedicated classes, and including special workshops. A fundamental's class in this case might be 45 minutes long, whereas a black belt class might run for 90 minutes.

Along with doing upgrade programmes, you can also sell your student new equipment or workshops to increase the size of purchase. We, as mentioned earlier, are always on the lookout for new bits of kit to add to our pro shop. We then run a special promotion and see if people are interested. If we get a positive feedback, we order in the new kit and do a big sales push.

Special workshops are also a good way to increase revenue. In every martial arts school, there are groups interested in specific topics. Your members may be interested in some or many of the following topics:

- Self-defence
- Fitness
- Sparring
- Competition
- Kicking
- Grappling
- Weapons

- Stretching
- Health
- Nutrition

To meet the needs of these particular people, you can organise short workshops on a particular topic and advertise it in your school. You will charge a small fee to attend the workshop, and if you get 20–30 people interested, it will prove lucrative.

But that's not the end of it. Some of the students will love what you covered and want to do more; in which case, you could run a six-week course, covering the topic in depth or suggest private lessons. Either way seminars can be a predictable source of income.

Another brilliant idea is to run a seminar that utilises a special piece of equipment. For example, we do a Thai pad seminar at our academy, and offer a pair of Thai pads at a reduced rate when you book onto the seminar.

This way you will sell a pair of Thai pads, the student get a set of Thai pads for less, and you also profit from the seminar fee.

Equipment packs are also another good way to increase the size of the average purchase, or you can upsell or cross sell. Upselling is offering the customer a larger size or better quality product. In a kickboxing club for example, you could have regular gloves and deluxe gloves. You give the customer the choice and tell them the benefits of both sets. Some people will be cost conscious and buy the cheaper gloves, and other people are quality conscious and only want the best, buying the deluxe versions. All you do is present the choice clearly.

Cross selling is offering additional products that complement the item they want to buy. The classic example is a burger and fries. You buy the burger, and the spotty teenager says, "Do you want fries with that?" and most people say "yes, go on then." That simple question earns McDonald's millions of pounds of extra revenue per year.

In the martial arts world, here are some classic cross-selling combinations:

- Gloves & pads
- Gloves & gum shield
- Gloves & hand wraps
- Gloves & head guard
- Shin guards & groin guard
- Sparring kit & bag to carry it all in

When a customer wants to buy some gloves, you can ask them if they want a set of pads to go with their gloves. Some will say yes, and some will say no. The reality is that they need both the gloves and pads, so you just ask them if they want to buy them now, rather than two months down the line.

Of course, this requires honesty and genuine respect for your customer. You are not a used car salesman trying to make a quick buck by adding on loads of unwanted extras. But, as you know, anyone who studies martial arts for any length of times needs the correct equipment to get the best from their training, so just offer them what they need.

3. INCREASE THE FREQUENCY OF PURCHASE.

Most people benefit from training at least twice week. Any less than that and they are not going to progress very far in terms of fitness or skill. As the student moves through the belts, we advise them to up their training as the gradings get harder and the fitness demands increase. Right before their black belt (which is a three-hour exam at our school), they should be training four times a week in preparation. We, therefore, have various prices based on how often students train. The more they train, the cheaper the classes are. This is a way of rewarding our most committed members. By moving them up the levels, we are helping them achieve their goals, but also asking them to buy more often.

You should also be running a series of seasonal promotions to encourage your customers to buy more frequently. Christmas is an obvious choice when people are on the lookout for presents, but it's also possible to sell fitness products and bootcamp type classes during the spring, leading up to summer. You have to think creatively to see how you can tie equipment sales to special events and seasonal promotions.

SEASONAL VARIATIONS IN THE MARTIAL ARTS INDUSTRY

Health and fitness are year-round efforts for the majority of people as health consciousness continues to increase across the country. However, I'm sure you are aware of the seasonal nature of martial arts training. For example, during the summer, class numbers decrease as many students go away on holidays for 2–6 weeks. The same thing happens at Christmas. So, although we as instructors are offering classes all year round, martial arts instruction is a seasonal industry. The busiest times for most schools is from early September (when the kids go back to school) through to the end of March. Those are the six peak months where most schools get the most new members joining.

Because of its seasonal nature, it's vital to have marketing activities in place during these peak moments, and also to have special promotions running during quieter times. If you miss the peak six months, you will spend the rest of the year trying to catch up. You need to have plans and strategies ready to take advantage of the times when your prospects are considering new fitness activities.

To summarise, if you want to make more money, you can increase your number of customers, increase the average size of a purchase, or increase the frequency of purchase, or do all three simultaneously.

LOCATION, LOCATION, LOCATION

This is term from the property industry that carries over into martial arts. If you open your school in the right location, you increase your chances of success. As a general rule, you want to open your classes in an affluent area with a high percentage of young families. This is because the major market for martial arts is kids and young adults. That's not to say there isn't a market for older adults, but it's just smaller. In most full-time schools, kids account for 50–70 per cent of the memberships. If you are not teaching kids, you are missing out. But that's your choice, and I understand that some instructors don't want to teach children. Young, health-conscious adults also like martial arts and enjoy the competitive parts of the arts. Finally middle-aged people do martial arts for the health and fitness benefits. If you can set up your club in an affluent residential area that contain these three groups, you will do well.

It definitely helps if the area you choose has households who earn above the national average income. This usually means that they have more disposable income and are willing to pay for special classes and clubs. If you don't live in an area like that, then you have two choices: set up where you are or go find a more affluent area. Having lived and taught in both places, I can tell you that setting up my club in a middle- to upper-income area was the single best business decision I ever made.

This is because my students can afford the training, don't try to haggle on price, are invested in improving themselves, buy equipment frequently, and are willing to pay for extra services like privates and seminars. This makes business relatively easy in such place, as long as you provide value and fully appreciate your customers.

My advice would be to do some research and find an affluent area local to you, with enough households to sustain your business, and think about opening there.

TARGETED MARKETING

You will want to appeal to children, mothers, and fathers from these affluent families in your chosen locale, who need exercise options that the family can share in a professionally run, yet friendly school.

You can split these families into four distinct groups:

1. Children under 10 yrs
2. Young adults from 11–15 yrs
3. Men from 16–55 yrs
4. Women, aged 16–55 yrs

You can then market to these groups, being aware that, frequently in many of these families, it is the mother who makes the buying decision. Your marketing therefore needs to be specifically targeted towards these mums, and what they desire for themselves, their children, and their partners/husbands.

Generally, in our experience, mums do not respond well to marketing that includes the following:

- Depictions of violence
- Aggression
- Images showing contact
- Mean-looking faces
- Sweaty bodies
- Too many pictures of men

So, if you have a pic of a sweaty guy, sitting on a guy and pounding his face in, on your marketing material, don't expect many mums (and, by extension, their families) in your classes. Generally, we use adverts and images that:

- Show happy people
- Usually in uniform
- Practicing some non-contact moves
- Well lit and bright pictures
- Worded to talk about the benefits for families

Your marketing should be targeted for the particular group you are trying to reach. Kids marketing should include words like the following:

Discipline, Self-confidence, Self-esteem, Bully defence, Control, Fun, Attention, Stranger danger.

Teen marketing should include these words:

Confidence, Body confidence, Healthy eating, Looking good, Peer pressure, Safety, Fitness, Weight control.

Adult marketing should use words to appeal to their health and well-being:

Fitness, Fat burning, Toning, Calorie burning, Weight loss, Stress release, Confidence, Self-defence.

Different groups require different key words/ images to motivate them to take action.

For example, an advert for teens that talks about "control, attention, and discipline" won't get much interest as teens aren't interested and, hopefully, already exhibit those qualities. But it will work for the mum or dad with a child, who needs help with those issues. So, choose your market correctly and get your message right, and you will be more successful.

TALK ABOUT THE BENEFITS OF TRAINING

This is a big problem that many martial artists have. I have lost count of the number of times I have seen this following scenario between a potential client, who walks into a studio, and an instructor:

Guy: Hi, I'm interested in learning XYZ martial arts.

Instructor: That's great, we have been doing XYZ for 15 years, won these titles, trained with this instructor, travelled to this country to learn it." (He goes into a long speech about the history of the style.)

Guy: Ummm, OK, that sounds ... interesting.

What's wrong with this conversation? It's all about the instructor, their style, their teachers, and their history. It's not about the guy who walked in.

Try this instead:

Guy: Hi, I'm interested in doing some XYZ style.

Instructor: Excellent and why's that?

Guy: Because I'm getting a bit overweight and out of shape.

Instructor: OK, I see, so you are looking to tone up a bit, get fit, and lose some weight. We can definitely help with that. Our classes focus on building fitness by ...

Which scenario puts the customer in a better frame of mind and makes him more receptive to your studio? No question about it. You quickly found out why he was there, told him you could help him, and he learnt about all about the benefits of training as they apply to him personally.

Here's another example:

Guy: Hi, I'm interested in learning XYZ style.

Instructor: Great and why's that?

Guy: Because I got mugged a couple of weeks back.

Instructor: Oh, that's terrible, what happened?

Guy: Well, this guy came out of nowhere ...

Instructor: I see. Well, we do teach XYZ, but I think that ABC may be a better place for you to start, seeing as you're looking for self-defence training.

By actively listening, we are able to ascertain our customer's needs and offer a solution that will actually help them. Frequently, I advise people not to do the martial arts they came in enquiring about, because I know it won't meet their needs. For example, I often get calls from prospects, asking about starting MMA to get in shape. Now, as you know MMA athletes are in ridiculous shape, but there is also a lot of technical training in an MMA class. I feel if people are primarily concerned with getting fit fast, Thai boxing would be a better choice than MMA. Thai boxing is easier to learn, with fewer techniques, it focuses on fitness and most people can pick up some rudimentary skills in the first few months.

LISTEN to what your prospect is saying either directly or indirectly, and help him or her to choose the right programme. I, for example, love MMA, have trained for it for 15 years, and fought professionally, but even I know it's not for everyone. If I don't feel a particular style will benefit a student, I advise them to try a different class.

So, try not to let your personal preferences distort your vision. Give the new student what he or she wants.

RETENTION

Once you have a happy stream of new prospects walking in the front door, you need to try to encourage them to stay around a while. Remember in martial arts, everyone quits. Yes, even you, but you will quit when you die.

For normal people, they will eventually stop because of injury, illness, boredom, moving away, work, family, or any other hundred reasons.

Your job as a martial arts instructor and business owner is to keep them training as long as possible. One, because it's in their interests to keep training to stay fit, healthy, balanced, flexible, stress free, focused, and disciplined. And secondly, it's also in your interests for them to continue, so you can pay your bills and build your business. Keeping students is called retention.

Retention comes down to keeping students interested, motivated, and continually benefiting from training martial arts. You keep students interested by doing these things:

1. Making your syllabus progressive
2. Making your classes fun and challenging
3. Building groups with your club
4. Setting long- and short-term goals
5. Appreciating students
6. Rewarding loyalty and dedication
7. Finding new challenges for them

MAKING YOUR SYLLABUS PROGRESSIVE

Many martial arts schools get their syllabus back to front. In that there is too much to learn at the beginning and not much left to learn at the end. That results in frustration for the beginner and boredom for the black belt. I recommend that your syllabus be the other way round. With our current syllabus there are only five techniques to learn for their first grade. Just five. New students should be able to learn these five techniques in a couple of weeks and then be ready to grade within four months. The point of this – baby steps and achievable goals.

Consider when you learnt to drive, your instructor didn't start your first lesson on the motorway; you started stationary and the instructor explained the controls of the car. The same applies in syllabus design: make it easy to succeed at the beginning, and build little victories in right from the start. If you over complicate things, you will lose a large percentage of your new students before they have even started. New students should feel competent after their very first session, and believe they can pick it up easily. Of course, we know they will struggle at times as the syllabus gets harder, but by that point they have built their confidence and self-belief.

You'd be surprised by how mentally fragile many people are. If they have a hard time picking something up or have to struggle with a technique, you might have already lost them. They have already decided that martial arts are too difficult, and they aren't coming back (even though they will tell you they are). Make their first few sessions so simple even a four-year-old child could do it. After a few months when they have joined the club, made a few friends, and completed their first grading, then you can increase the complexity. But, personally, I save all the really difficult stuff till after black belt.

At the other end of the spectrum, a common reason why many people quit after black belt is that they have achieved a long-held goal, and they don't have anything to replace it with. In my system, a black belt is someone who understands the basics of martial arts. They are not a master or an expert. The just have solid fundamentals.

All the cool technical stuff is taught after black belt. By this point, they should be very confident and up for the challenge, so blow their minds then, not in their second class.

MAKE YOUR CLASSES FUN AND CHALLENGING

You probably stuck with martial arts for such a long time because you enjoyed it. I only really train for enjoyment now. I have done all the crazy cage-fighting stuff, and now just train for the joy it brings me. Well, your students are no different. They want to enjoy their training and have fun. If your classes are boring, overly repetitive, or too serious, then you are taking some of the fun out of their training.

Repetition is the foundation of skill, but it doesn't mean you have to repeat a move in exactly the same way every lesson. A round kick can be taught in many different ways in order to add a bit of variety to a class:

- Power round kick
- Speed round kick
- Spinning round kick
- Jumping round kick
- Switch round kick
- Missed round kick to spin kick
- Round kick on pads
- Round kick on paddles
- Round kick on shield
- Round kick sparring
- And so on...

We know the student is still practicing the same round kick, but to them it's new and totally different. Therefore, they enjoy training the new variation. This is called disguised repetition. You find 20 ways to teach a technique and use a different one each week. Using disguised repetition keeps students training a lot longer than doing the same thing in the same way. Fun classes also have an element of the unexpected.

Sometimes we will do pad drills with the lights off to simulate a self-defence situation; sometimes we do drills on our knees to learn how to generate power with our upper bodies only. Other times, we have big gang fights where everyone spars everyone (light contact, of course). This is a great drill to develop 360 degree awareness and street smarts. We only do these "fun drills" now and then, but they get the students talking and excited. Enthusiastic and excited students stay around longer.

ENCOURAGING THE DEVELOPMENT OF GROUPS WITH YOUR CLUB

People naturally like to form social groups wherever they go. It's human nature to like and hang out with people who are similar to you. In a martial arts schools, you will get the following common groups:

1. Fighters

If you train fighters or competitive athletes, this group will meet and start to form a common bond. The fighters will hang out together, swap war stories, share tips, and generally have a good time. Encourage this by organising specific training for fighters only. Run seminars for fighters only, go to events as a group, print a club fighter's only T-shirt. Fighter focused events will reinforce this group and keep them training.

2. Fitness fanatics

This group of super-fit individuals likes to train hard, go to the gym, do extra training after class, and hang out with other fitness nuts. Keep them happy by offering fitness-focused classes, setting fitness challenges as part of your gradings, running bootcamp-type workshops, and entering them as a team into fitness events like the Tough Mudder.

3. Technique junkies

This crowd likes collecting cool techniques and creating lists of things they know.

They devour anything new, buy new training DVDs, and take lots of notes. Keep them happy by doing a lot of seminars on different topics, having a challenging syllabus, organising seminars with guest instructors, and running dedicated black belt classes.

4. Socialites

These people like the social aspect of martial arts. They are always hanging around chatting to everyone after class or are on Facebook, making comments. Keep them happy by organising social events, trips, fight-nights, picnics, and parties. Get them discussing stuff on Facebook.

If you can help all these groups and provide fun activities for each, you will retain more students. A martial arts school is not 300 individuals, it's a collection of small groups that interact to a degree, but have their own special rules and behaviours.

SETTING LONG- AND SHORT-TERM GOALS

We used to have a problem with students quitting after black belt. After much thought and analysis, we worked out that it was because the gradings changed from every four months before black belt to yearly after black belt. This was a problem.

Our students were used to having short-term goals in the not too distant future. By tripling the time between gradings, we left them without a short-term goal and they drifted away. The solution was to modularise the black belt dan gradings. This means that they do a module (or part of their grading) every six months to give them a short-term goal. Once they have completed enough modules, they were awarded their next dan grade. This worked wonders with our 30 black belts, who are now working happily towards their next short-term goal.

Everyone needs short- and long-term goals. In martial arts, we have the black belt as a long-term goal that motivates 95 per cent of our students to commit to 3–10 years of weekly training. The belt system is used to set short-term goals on the way to the black belt test. You can't go straight from white belt to black belt. There are 4–10 other belts to earn first. Which is great, as the other belts act as markers along the road to mastery. For this reason, it is advisable to really focus on the importance of grading at your schools.

If your students get the impression that you are not bothered by gradings, neither will they be. Everything comes down from the top. If you are always excited by and talking about black belt goals and gradings, your students will also appreciate its importance and follow your lead.

In my experience there are two groups of students not interested in grading: fighters and fitness fanatics. Fighters like to fight and test themselves through combat.

Short-term goals for a fighter might be improving in sparring or winning an interclub event. Long-term goals include titles, trophies, and the glory of war.

Fitness fanatics also tend not to care about grading. You will need to set some pretty intense fitness goals to keep them motivated. I'm sure you have some pretty tough fitness tests that you put your students through, so refine, modify, or steal some more. Design some fiendish challenges that will keep them training hard and coming back for more. Putting up a fitness leaderboard also motivates this type of person to keep striving to beat the competition.

APPRECIATING STUDENTS

The times I haven't appreciated my students have bit me on the ass. I once got a little lazy and indifferent and before I knew it, I had lost dozens of students. Lesson learnt BIG TIME. I am now extremely grateful for my students, as they allow me to live my life expressing my passion and achieving my dreams. Anytime you take your students for granted, you're putting your business in jeopardy. They will slowly pick up on your lack of interest and start drifting away to someone who does care.

Every day you need to let your students know that you value them and appreciate the time and money they spend with you.

Here are some ways to show your appreciation.

1. Say Thanks

Say "thank you" to your students in person (which is best), on the phone, via text, email, or carrier pigeon. Just make sure they know that you are thankful for their continued support.

2. Know their names

It's hard to be thankful when you haven't even bothered learning their names. Try to learn all your students' names. Nothing indicates a lack of respect more than calling everyone "mate." You probably won't remember all your students' names, but you should try.

3. Help them out

Occasionally, we get a call from a student who can't afford to pay for a while, due to work or family problems. If we were mercenary, we would send them on their way. Instead, we prefer to come to a deal that allows them to continue training till they have their finances in order. Maybe, they can help out in exchange for classes, deliver flyers for you, or mop the mats. Or, perhaps, you could say, "Don't worry about your fees this month, start paying again next month."

4. Run free events now and then

As a reward for your students loyalty, run a free workshop now and then. Tell them it's to say thanks for being wonderful students.

5. Give a gift

If a student does something great for you off their own back, maybe buy them a little gift to say "thank you."

6. Feed them

I regularly take my coaches and assistants out for a meal on me to say thanks for helping build a wonderful business. It's really the least I can do. Maybe, you can do the same?

7. Rewarding loyalty and dedication

Loyalty is a funny thing in martial arts. Many instructors demand it, which usually backfires on them. My first instructor, Grandmaster Anton St'James, always made it clear that we could train with whoever we liked to continue our journey. He was cool like that. It's like when you were a kid leaving home, the door was always open for you to come back anytime you wanted. This was great, and that's why he is still my instructor and inspiration to this day.

Loyalty can be rewarded in many ways. You can actively thank a student in person for his or her support. You can do the same in front of a class and watch them fill with pride. You can do it by email. You could give a little certificate or plaque at your Christmas party or just send them a nice bunch of flowers or bottle of wine with a note. However you do it, it's enough to say thanks for sticking with me.

Dedication is easy to recognise. Whenever a student reaches a certain milestone, whether it be for one, three, five, or ten years training, recognise it and congratulate them publicly. We have even got a special uniform for students who have completed ten years training.

8. Finding new challenges for them

This can be a tricky one, as you have to know your students well to notice when they are losing motivation. Usually, there are a few key indicators. For example, they start missing classes, don't attend special events or workshops, and don't seem excited by training. Urgent action is needed. You need to have a chat with them and find out what's going on. Don't interrogate, just ask and listen. Once you know how they feel, discuss setting some new goals with them. These can include several approaches.

a) Fitness goals

Can they complete a certain number of exercises in a certain time? Do they want to lose a certain amount of body fat? Also keep a fitness leaderboard displayed in your school, so people can see who the champ is.

b) Training goals

Is there a grading coming up or do they want to master a particular technique or drill? Set some difficult goals that force them to stretch and work harder.

c) Coaching goals

Can they help a beginner through to their next belt? This is called mentoring, where a senior student takes a junior under their wing and guides them. This can create strong bonds in your school.

d) Business goals

If they run their own schools, what goals can you help them develop? An extra 50 students, a full-time centre, black belt assistants, or more profit?

e) Competition goals

Some people love competition and thrive in that environment. If they don't have any major competitions coming up, then how about a few smaller local comps to keep their hand in and, hopefully, win some gold?

f) Social goals

Do they want to organise a few social events? Some students love organising fun outings and events. Let them do what they love.

Try to find out what floats their boat, and then set some short- and long-term goals. They need to find their passion again, so do your utmost to reignite that spark or you will lose them.

If you do these retention strategies consistently, you will find that your students stay longer and train harder. It's up to you as the leader to invest the energy and keep your students training as long as possible. The other way to keep students is by reducing attrition.

ATTRITION

Attrition is the opposite of retention; it's what makes students quit. When you ask a student why they stopped, their answer usually falls into one of two categories: reasons under your control, and reasons not under your control.
Reasons for quitting not under your control (for example, there is nothing you can do about the following):

- Work commitments
- Family responsibilities
- Job changes (Unemployment)
- Moving to a different location
- Reasons for quitting which are under your control:
- Injury
- Lack of exciting goals
- Boredom
- Not having fun

INJURY

Injuries happen in martial arts, but a lot of the time, they can be avoided. Slight bumps and bruises are to be expected in a combat sport, but serious ligament or tendon injuries are to be avoided at all costs. As an instructor, part of your job is to protect the students from themselves, and this involves:

MONITORING SPARRING SO IT DOESN'T GET OUT OF CONTROL

Sparring can escalate really quickly. One student gets hit a bit harder than they were expecting, bites down on their gum shield and starts swinging back. Before you know it, World War 3 starts. To prevent this, you need to pre-frame the whole class on acceptable contact levels. At our school, we allow hard contact to the legs and body, and light to medium impact to the head. This is to protect the brain as 95 per cent of our students don't fight competitively, so hard contact to the head is unnecessary. They also tend to have high-powered jobs in the City in London, and don't want to go in to work with a black eye and broken nose. That seems reasonable to me, so we control contact to the head. The forfeit for losing control is 25 burpees and a round on the bag to calm down. That generally sorts them out, and prevents any serious injuries during sparring.

SUGGESTING ALTERNATIVES FOR STUDENT WITH INJURIES

Many students have pre-existing conditions or injuries. When they fill in their PAR-Q, you should be able to assess what they can and cannot do, but you still need to ask. A student with an injured knee shouldn't be doing plyometric leg exercises, for example. A student with a shoulder injury should maybe avoid punching drills in case of aggravating it.

You need to be aware of the students in the class with injuries and give them safer alternatives, or you will be helping the student to quit when their injury gets worse.

This is why before EVERY class I teach I ask:

Does anyone have any injuries or illnesses I should know about?

Usually a few hands go up, and I can modify my lesson plan for these people.

If you don't ask this question, they will do whatever the class is doing and hurt themselves. Generally, if the person has a lower-body injury, you give them upper body drills and exercises and vice versa.

CHECKING THE TRAINING SPACE ON THE LOOKOUT FOR COLLISIONS, ETC.

If you have busy classes, you will need to be extra aware of issues with space and collisions. People have a pretty low awareness of space and can crash into each other easily. You need to watch out for students running into many things including:

- Each other
- Walls
- Mirrors
- Equipment (hanging bags, etc.)
- Reception area

Kids are the worst for this. They just run about looking the wrong way and go straight into a wall. We have padded our walls for this exact reason. If you have bare walls and teach busy classes, you might also consider padding or try to put a barrier of some sort between the wall and the class.

CONTROLLING CONTACT

Students have different ideas of acceptable contact. To some people, a light brush is too hard, while with others, you can kick them full power and they just blink. This is not a problem, unless they are matched together during class, and then it's a nightmare. The person, who dislikes contact, gets hit, injured, and put off martial arts for life. This may sound silly, but I have lost several students as a result of this.

Some people are more sensitive than others, and may get upset if there receive too much impact. So, you have to match partners VERY carefully. I find it a good idea to agree about contact levels between students before they start drilling.

Let's say they are doing a low kick to the leg drill. They exchange light kicks and gradually up the contact till they are both happy. Encourage students to speak up if they are concerned about excessive contact.

MATCHING PARTNERS WELL

I'm a constantly surprised by the weird choices people make when partnering up in the class. You know, the 15 stone guy with the 8 stone woman? I always check who is partnered with who and swap bad matches. You always want to match like with like:

- Women with women
- Men with men
- Big with big
- Small with small
- High skill with high skill
- Fit with fit
- Calm with calm
- And so on

Mismatching people will lead to frustration and anger, with students quitting when they get injured. If you can't get an exact match, put the student on a punch bag or get an assistant to pair up with them as well.

If you do these things, the rate of injury will go down at your school, and that means a higher retention rate, which is always good for your business.

GOALS

We have already talked about setting goals with students. Try to get them to commit to a goal and follow up with them regularly to check that they are on target. Don't let them off the hook. They need to be kept accountable.
If a student wants to be able to do 50 press-ups, keep checking in with him or her and offer tips and advice.

BOREDOM

Boredom can happen. As a black belt, we realise that boredom is part and parcel of success. We have spent hours drilling the same move to make it part of our nervous system.

But as black belts, we are in the minority, since most people get bored by repetition.

There are two schools of thought about this problem: The first school says, "Tough" get focused and keep training. The other school thinks, "OK, let's see if we can vary this in some way to make it interesting, but maintain its core integrity."

In my experience, if you want students to train for 10–20 years, you will need to get creative in the ways that you deliver the material. After all there are only so many ways you can move the human body. That is why I keep learning new martial arts and studying the latest developments in the fitness industry. This helps me come up with new ideas and approaches, and is why we have so many students training past black belt.

Dare I say it – but you can also go on YouTube and search for something like "Pressup

Variations" and find 50 videos, showing loads of cool variations you can use in your class today. Obviously, learning martial arts off YouTube is very difficult if not impossible, but you can pick up loads of good tips around:

- Fitness drills
- Exercises variations
- Circuit training
- Stretching
- Partner drills

- Balancing exercises
- Plyometric exercises
- Kid's games

LACK OF FUN

Fun to me can mean using humour, variety, or the unexpected whilst teaching. I have a very relaxed teaching style, so I crack a lot of jokes and enjoy my time with my students.

Fun helps people to relax and makes them more receptive to learning new things. And we love chucking in the unexpected. For example, in a kickboxing class we might add some MMA ground & pound training to spice things up. In the MMA class, we might get people to grapple with a training knife to understand the realities of grappling with weapons. And in the weapons class, we might integrate some of the kicking from the Thai boxing class. You can mix and cross arts like this, and it always gets students excited. Excited students are happy students.

INDIFFERENCE

One of the major cause of students quitting is indifference from instructors. This means the student doesn't feel like the instructor cares about them or their goals. We have all had the experience of going into a shop, and the person serving is chatting or not attentive. After a few seconds, I get really angry. I'm standing there holding my money wanting to pay, and they're laughing away with their co-workers clearly ignoring me. I usually put down whatever I was going to buy and leave, and never use that shop again. We don't like poor customer service, so why would we treat our students like that?

Our students are the most important people in the world while we are teaching. You should bend over backwards to help them where possible. They will quit eventually anyway, but you are extending the time they will stay with you and creating a lot of goodwill by treating them respectfully.

MISSING IN ACTION CALLS

To check what's going on with a student, first, you need to note their absence from class. This is why you need a register, a card system, or attendance tracking software. You can't catch up with a student if you don't know they are missing. So once you have noted their absence for more than seven days get in contact. I used to call students who went MIA (missing in action), but now I text them instead. It's easier and quicker, and people are more likely to get back to you. You just send the following text to get a conversation going:

"Hi (name). We haven't seen you in class lately, we hope everything is OK, and we will see you back soon." Best wishes (your name)."

Nine out of ten times, you get a text back the same day explaining the absence. Reply and try to get them to commit to a day when they will return.

Try to say something like this:

"Great, which day do you think you will be in next week?"

This forces them to try to turn up as they know you are expecting them.

Finish you text conversation along these lines:

"Excellent, I will see you on Tuesday at 7.30 p.m. then. Look forward to it (your name)."

This usually get students back to training pretty quickly. If you have a grading approaching, you could also mention that.

"Hope to see you back soon as we have a grading in six weeks, and you're hopefully going for your next belt."

CANCELLATIONS CALLS

Some students don't give you any indication that they are dissatisfied and then they just cancel. Try to give them a call on the day that they cancel to find out what has changed in their lives. The problem with this is rarely will they tell you, their instructor, the truth. They may have hated every second of training, but they will claim it's because their cat died. So, you may have to do a little digging to find out their real reasons.

It's a good idea to ask if it's about money as many people are embarrassed to admit they cannot afford something. Or, you may have to ask their classmates,

"Hey, what happened to Andrew; he was doing really well?" Then you find out that he got beaten up in sparring, and it put him off.

Try to find out the real reason why someone cancelled, and then do something about it. We regularly do special reduced rates or offer free 30-minute privates to help get people back to class.

CHECKING OUT THE COMPETITION

People like variety, and they like to check out the competition. If you see this as a problem then you'd best skip this chapter. We have several martial arts school and boxing clubs near our location. While we don't actively encourage our students to leave and try out these places, if they do, we let them go happily and tell them they are welcome back anytime.

Invariably, they return with stories of poor customer service and apathy from the competition. This then strengthens their relationship with your business as they realise you are the real deal. Occasionally, we actively tell our students to try training with another instructor. There comes a point where your advanced students need to find their own way and test the waters elsewhere. If you try to hold onto them too hard, they start resisting and pulling way.

Encourage them to go, but always remind them that they are welcome back at any time. Most return and bring new insight and fresh approaches.

There will also be students who are very gifted, and you cannot teach them anymore as you have reached your limits. You should always advise them to go and find a new instructor. They will thank you forever for your humility and honesty, and refer you new clients. Finally, the instructors I know who try to control their students typically have less than 30, and they always leave eventually, usually after having a flaming row. Like the saying goes:

"If you love someone, you must set them free."

HANDLING COMPLAINTS

Studies have shown that if you handle a complaint well, you actually can increase loyalty in the person complaining. People like to know that their feelings are being taken seriously, and will respond positively to anyone who cares enough and puts them first. Certain instructors have no time for this: "it's my way or the highway."

But in today's social-media-driven world, this can be business suicide.
Let's say you are rude and publicly embarrass someone who makes a legitimate complaint. First of all, you have lost a customer for life, and 20 years ago they would have told all their friends not to use your business. With the advent of social media, they will now tell their 500 friends on Facebook. These friends will also discuss and share your failings for your entire local community to see.

What is even worse is that they will post their complaints on your business fan page for all your prospects to see. Or, they will post a three-page terrible critique of your business, and it will stay in the search engines forever. These days you need to handle complaints very professionally in the following way:

1. You need to listen to the complaint in its entirety without interrupting.

2. Then you need to repeat the problem back to the person in their own words to check that you have got it right.

3. After that you need to apologise for any hurt you may have caused (even if you didn't intend or realise you caused any).

4. Next you need to offer to make it right.

5. Then you make it right and check that they are happy with the outcome.

Do all this with genuine respect for your customer, and you will create a fan who will post on Facebook saying what a top person you are and how you care for your customers. Handling complaints professionally takes training and patience, but it will pay off big time and get you many raving fans, so take it seriously.

REACTIVATING PAST CUSTOMERS WITH AN IRRESISTIBLE OFFER

For students that are leaving or have left, it is possible to reactivate them with a special offer. Every year, I email the few thousand (yes, thousand) people who have stopped training with us, with an irresistible offer. This could be an offer for free training for an extended period, a special discounted rate, or a new equipment pack when they re-join.

Whatever your offer, it has to be really tempting to get someone off their butt and back into your school. Two weeks free won't cut it. We are talking about three months free training here. It has to be so good that they would be a total fool not to take you up on it. If they do take up your irresistible offer, make sure you welcome them back with open arms, make them feel special, and communicate with them via text or email to see how they are doing.

LESSON PLANNING

Lesson planning is a key skill in retention. Unplanned lessons tend to be disorganised, repetitive or random, disjointed, and not as fun. The problem with "winging it" is that you have to make stuff up on the spot. Sometimes that stuff is freaking awesome, but more often than not, it's just dull. Five minutes planning before every class will quickly improve the quality of your sessions significantly.

That even goes if you have been teaching for 20 years like me. The lessons I plan always go smoother and are more enjoyable and less stressful. Our lesson plans have five distinct sections.

1. Pre-frame and announcements

This is where we tell the students what to expect during the class. This way they can mentally prepare themselves and get in the zone. People like to know what to expect. We also give announcements of upcoming events, seminars, and gradings.

2. Warm-up

Every practice should begin with a warm-up that takes 8 to 15 minutes. Warming-up your body before exercising produces many benefits that can help a person achieve maximum value from martial arts training.

The amount of time spent on the warm-up will vary depending on these factors:

a. The fitness level of the class

b. Age of the students

c. Type of martial arts program (beginner, intermediate, advanced, sparring, etc.)

d. Type of equipment available

e. Workout-area size

f. Temperature of the room

g. Gender

Warming-up is vital. A local school recently got sued by a woman who injured herself as a result of not warming-up properly.

3. Main Class

After the warm-up comes the main body of the class. This usually (at our gym) includes the following:

- Well-matched partner drills (5 minutes)
- Pad work or bag work (20 minutes)
- Fitness exercises (10 minutes)
- Optional sparring (10 minutes)

Partner drills

Partner drills are practicing techniques with a partner to develop skills. We usually go one for one on a particular technique or combination.

Pad work

Pad work or bag work lets people actually apply the drill they have just done with full power and intensity. This is the part of training most people enjoy. It gets them sweating and builds their fitness.

4. Fitness training

We usually use body weight exercise like press-ups, sit-ups, squats, and burpees in combination to develop strength, endurance, and muscular fitness. Beginners do low reps, and experienced people do as many reps as possible. We also include a lot of variation in exercise selection, so that people don't get bored. Try to keep everything fresh and interesting. Don't do the same pattern of exercises every class. Create a list of different types of push-ups, sit-ups, and squats, and change it up in every class.

Optional sparring

Some people like to spar and some don't. Give them the choice by making sparring optional. We expect our students to be able to spar, but don't require it in every session. Some may prefer to work on the bags or build their fitness.

5. High-energy finish

After the main session comes the high-energy finish. This is a quick five-minute burst of high-energy exercise that is designed to have everyone leave on an endorphins high. We used to do a long stretch at the end of class, but noticed that people were leaving tired and cold. So, we changed to a high-energy finish, as a result they go home feeling pumped up. The high-energy finish can be a bag drill or an intense fitness blast or a combination of both. It should only last five minutes though.

Thank them

At the end of the class, bow the students out and thank them for attending.

Spotlight a few people who impressed you during class, and hang around on the mat to answer questions and dispense wisdom.

Lesson planning

The best way to write an entire lesson plan is on a sheet of A4 paper for every lesson either at the beginning of the week or right before the class starts. While this seems very time consuming to start with, after a year, you will have over 100 lesson plans written out. You can then select the best, and keep 30 or so in a folder at your academy to use over and over.

The other advantage of written lesson plans is that you can share them with your instructors and assistants. There are times when you might need another instructor to take a class. If you let them do whatever they fancy, don't be surprised if you get some very weird things being taught. One night in one of our kickboxing classes, I caught an instructor teaching head-butts. Head-butting, in a kickboxing class?

Maybe that's appropriate for a self-defence class, but definitely not kickboxing. We had a quiet word. It's far better to ask them to cover, and then give them a pre-prepared lesson plan and say, "please teach ONLY this." Then you know exactly what is being taught, and you can monitor results. As long as they follow the plan, they can't go wrong.

Make sure everyone, including yourself, creates written lesson plans for every class.

Taking care of yourself

The problem with running your own martial arts business is that initially you are doing everything in the business. You are the:

- Instructor
- Manager
- Receptionist
- Cleaner
- Marketer
- Website designer
- Printer
- Dog's body
- Delivery driver
- Counsellor
- And more

This means that it is very easy to burn out if you don't manage your energy well. This is especially true if you also have a demanding day job. To avoid burnout, you need to focus on high-importance activities first ¬– that is the things that make the biggest difference to your business. Let's say you have three things on your to-do list:

1. Pick up equipment from suppliers.
2. Return calls to prospects.

3. Distribute flyers to local shops.

The most important item on that list is the one that is going to earn you money, and that is calling your prospects back. Next comes distributing flyers and last is picking up the equipment. Marketing activities should always come first, as they are what bring and keep people at your school. So learn how to prioritise your to-do list.

Ask yourself, what on this list is going to earn you the most income and do that first!

However, even when you are prioritising well, you are likely to still feel overwhelmed, so it's important to include regenerative activities into your schedule. Otherwise, you will be rushing around all day – doing, doing, doing – and, before you know it, you haven't eaten, taken a break, or relaxed all day. This is unsustainable; eventually you will burn out, get ill or have a meltdown (like I did).

As a business owner in order to be successful, you may have to work much harder than the average employee does. At points, you might need to put in 60+ hours a week to get to where you want to be. So being smart and taking time out to recharge is vital. Here are my favourite recharging activities:

1. Walk in nature.

A quick walk in nature calms your frazzled nerves, gets you breathing, and settles the mind. 10–20 minutes is all it takes.

2. Power Nap.

Put your feet up, put the phone on answer phone or preferably use call answering, and have a nap. These power naps are a lifesaver when you are tired and stressed. Try not to nap for more than 30 minutes, as any longer will mess with your sleep pattern at night.

3. Gentle exercise.

This doesn't mean whacking out ten rounds on the bag, but more of a mobilisation and stretch like yoga. Move your body, stretch your neck, loosen off, and after ten minutes get back to work.

4. Massage.

Yep that's right go get a massage. Back, neck, and shoulders are perfect for weary school owners. It helps relieve tension, soothes the mind, and feels good.

Of course you could just ignore my advice and down a can of red bull instead, but this is a very short-term solution to a long-term problem. Caffeine works but it has a negative effect on the body, and can become addictive, so don't rely on it.

Set up a mastermind group

One of the best things I have ever done for my business is to set up my own mastermind group. This is a group of like-minded individuals who share ideas, help each other, offer advice, and keep you honest. Being a business owner can be a very lonely place. You have to cope with a lot of stress and uncertainty, and having a support group is valuable. You can set up a mastermind group on Facebook or any social media site.

Just invite a few fellow martial artists and business owners and get chatting. Any topic is up for discussion, successes, failures, warnings, problems and guidance.

Everyone gives their opinion and shares their experiences. It's really useful to get other peoples perspective when you are struggling with a problem. We also get together in person several times a year to plan and catch up. It's a very positive experience, and since I set up my mastermind group, my business has gone from strength to strength.

Business priorities

As mentioned it is very important to prioritise the most important tasks for your business so that they get done. Everything else will have to wait or be delegated. In my opinion, the top three things you should be doing everyday are getting new students, teaching great classes, and learning about business.

During the early stages of your business, you should do the following three activities every day:

1. Marketing (to get new students).

Do the marketing minimums and some of the extra marketing activities discussed every day. If you have time, aim for two hours a day marketing. If you don't have that much time, do at least an hour a day. Make it a daily habit to find and create new customers.

2. Teaching awesome classes (to keep students).

Students need to be sweating, smiling, and learning at every class. If you are having a bad day, leave it at the door. If you take a foul mood into class, it can ruin an entire session and push people over the edge, and make them quit. Be upbeat, positive, and focused when teaching. Plan all your lessons in advance.

3. Learning (the skills you need to run your business).

In the beginning, you are your business. Therefore, any weaknesses your business has are caused by you. To strengthen your business you need to learn as much as you can about marketing, sales, systems, customer service and more. As you get smarter, you will start making better choices and understand the business implications of the choices you make.

Try to read a business book a week. Start on something light like an autobiography on a business personality you respect and build from there. Many business books can be dry and boring, but some are excellent. I have listed my favourite business books at the end of this book.

If you prefer to listen to stuff, then Audible is an Amazon company that sells audiobooks, which you can download to your iPod, iPhone, or Android device. They have a great range of audio business books, and their prices are very reasonable.

If you are more visually inclined, you can watch DVDs or TED talks. I have also listed a few of my favourite stage speakers, who work well in that medium, at the end of this book.

Once you have built up a solid student base and have trained some class assistants, you can start delegating.

4. Delegating (so you can focus on key tasks).

Make it part of your instructor training programme to help assist in classes; this benefits your assistants as they get to practice teaching, and it takes some of the load off of you. We usually start our assistant instructor training by having them take a warm-up, and then keep building them gradually, until they can teach an entire class on their own. You will need to monitor them the entire time, but it will take some of the responsibility off you to teach all of the classes. Make sure you comprehensively train and insure all your assistant instructors.

5. Systematising (so you can train more people to do more stuff).

A lot of the things you do in your business take a lot of time and effort. If you can write down or film how to do them, you can train someone else to do it for you. For example, if you teach an assistant how to take equipment orders, they can do so while you attend to new students or answer questions. By having everything written down, it decreases the chance of anyone making a mistake. They just follow the instructions. This ensures you will get the outcome you desire, and it makes life simpler for everyone.

6. Optimising (testing and improving what you are already doing).

As your business stands, it will be doing some things poorly, some things well, and a few things amazingly. You need to find out what is happening in every area of your business. Test everything and bring up all the levels. Let's say you have poor conversion from phone calls to intro lesson (meaning that not many students book an intro lesson after speaking to you on the phone). You will need to improve that area by looking at what is said during the calls and testing a new approach or script.

Once you have a team of people working for you, and you have systematised and optimised, the next step to come is innovation:

7. Innovate (coming up with new ideas and strategies).

All businesses need to innovate to stay current and ahead of the competition. As you know martial arts is continually evolving, and so is business. What worked ten years ago doesn't work now. This is evident with the explosion of MMA. There were only a handful of MMA clubs when I first started competing and today there are probably two or three in every large town. Of course, MMA will be overtaken in a few years by the next big thing.

That's not to say you need to be faddish and copy the latest craze, but you need to be aware of what it is, how it works, and how you can ride the wave to use it to your advantage. Using MMA, for example, you don't need to drop all your traditional classes and start teaching MMA, but you could create an MMA fitness class using your traditional skills. You also need to stay ahead of the curve in business as well.

Social media is a big thing right now, and you need to have a social-media presence and a following to help build your school. But who knows what will happen in five years' time, so keep up to date.

If you think some new technology has value, try to be an early adopter, so you can benefit from being ahead of the pack. This means reading about the latest trends in our industry, researching new developments in marketing, and speaking to business owners in other fields to see what unique ideas they have. Innovation also involves coming up with new ways to improve your business yourself. Funnily enough, these "light bulb" moments tend not to happen when you are teaching, but frequently happen when you are doing something else entirely.

For example, I had the light bulb moment about modularising the black belt gradings whilst I was painting a wall. This is why time out is important, as it allows you to process and mull over ideas until your subconscious comes up with a solution

.

8. Replicate (if you want to recreate your success with a chain of satellite schools).

Once you have a working model and written systems, it is possible to replicate your school. This usually involves asking a student, who wants to teach, if they would be interested in setting up a satellite school using your systems, processes, and brand.

If they are interested, you will need to decide how you both want to structure things like payments, systems, intellectual property, licences to use the business systems, etc. It is important to have a written agreement in place, so there is no chance of misunderstanding at any point. This will need to be drafted by a solicitor or a company like NEST, which has agreements already written that can be modified to be used in your business.

It's always better to have everything in black and white from the start, so that everyone knows where they stand. There is nothing worse than falling out with a student over money. It sucks and leaves a bad taste in everyone's mouth. If everything is agreed in writing before you start working together, then any problems can be resolved by referring back to the original agreement. Written agreements may seem weird and are not common in the martial arts field, but if you have created a unique system that will enable a student to build a profitable business, then you need to protect your property, brand and business.

9. Monitor everything in your business – test and plan.

If you don't monitor everything in your business, you will be fighting blind. You need to keep your eye on how everything performs: from your marketing right through to how the classes are taught. Remember your KPI's and systematise as much as possible. If you want to try a new process or product, then test it first, and, if it outperforms your control, adopt it.

If you want to try a new flyer design or banner on your website or phone script, you have to split test and see which version performs best. Then you have to test everything live with your prospects. In my experience your personal biases will frequently be wrong. Let your prospects choose what works.

To give you an example, I set up a website to sell pad training videos, called www.mittmaster.com. I personally prefer to download training videos and thought everyone was the same as me. I sold a few online videos, but not as many as I wanted. On a whim, I put all the online videos onto a physical DVD and it sold out immediately. If I had ignored my own preferences and split tested the digital download vs. DVD, I wouldn't have wasted a year's worth of time, energy, and money. You can split test everything in your business:

- Phone call scripts
- Intro lesson structure
- Class times

- Training fees
- Payment methods
- Instructors
- Equipment prices
- Grading times
- Systems
- Rewards
- Syllabi
- Uniforms
- T-shirt designs
- Instructor training
- Flyer design
- Website banners
- Sales copy

YOUR COMPETITIVE EDGE OVER YOUR COMPETITION

Hopefully, this book has made you think about what is unique about your business when compared to your competitors. What makes you different/ superior to your competition is your Unique Sales Position (USP).

To give you an example, here are my school's USP's.

USP: Full-time Academy

This makes us rare and helps people take us more seriously as a business. We present ourselves as a professional full-time school.

USP: Varied Timetable

We offer over 35 classes per week: classes for kids, teens, adults, ladies only, MMA, and BJJ classes. This is a wide range of classes to offer and makes us able to target many different niche groups.

USP: Martial Arts Experience

Both my partner, James, and I have trained for over 25 years and fought professionally, which improves our creditability. Plus, we have a team of black belt instructors, who have over a decade's experience each. This creates authority in the minds of potential prospects.

USP: Excellent Student to Instructor Ratio (1–7 in classes for kids and 1–10/15 in adult classes)

We try to maintain a low student to instructor ratio. We have seen classes at other schools with sixty students and a lone instructor. I have no idea how this works, but we prefer to keep our classes smaller and more personal. We feel this is better for our students as they get more individual attention. We also have assistants in every class helping out.

USP: Separate Classes for Kids, Teenagers, and Adults

This is vital in my opinion. We would never have kids and adults training in the same class. There is a conflict of interest when this happens. Kids and adults have different needs and should be taught in different ways. Putting them all together in one class is not beneficial for either group. And that's without the risks of injury with small kids and big adults in the same space. Separate your classes if you can.

USP: Assistant Instructors in all Children's Classes

This helps enormously as assistants can sort out a range of problems while you focus on teaching the class.

USP: Wide Variety of Free Equipment for Students to Use.

We have a lot of equipment that students get to use during their sessions, including the following:

- Punch bags
- Ground & pound bags
- Kick shields
- Focus mitts
- Thai pads
- Gloves
- Skipping ropes
- Hand weights
- Kick paddles
- Resistance bands
- Medicine balls

- Kettle bells

This is attractive to new students as they can play with new toys, but also makes classes more interesting as instructors can use different pieces of equipment whilst teaching.

USP: All Chief Instructors Have Degrees in Sport Science

Both my business partner and I have a BSc in Sports Science, which really establishes our credibility as instructors and experts in our field.

USP: Safe, Friendly, yet Professional Environment.

We make sure training is as safe as possible whilst being fun. The floors and walls are matted. All instructors have insurance and are DBS checked.

USP: We have female instructors, which opens up the women's only market.

Thankfully, a lot more women are starting martial arts, and by having female instructors teaching this appeals to women interested in starting.

USP: Space and Time for Private Lessons / Seminars.

We can give students a more personalised training experiences by offering private lessons and seminars.

USP: Centrally Located Between Major Towns and Easy to Find

We are located between three major towns and have good access via road and tube.

USP: Free Parking

Everyone travels by car, so we made sure we have plenty of parking spaces outside our academy. We can easily accommodate thirty cars at night.

All these factors help people choose our school over our competition. Marketing is about educating your prospects, so that they can make an informed choice. By using this information in our marketing, we can create a compelling argument of why we are the only viable choice for martial arts instruction in our area. While other schools may have one, two, or more of these advantages, they don't have them all, and this elevates our school above the pack.

OUR WEAKNESSES COMPARED TO THE COMPETITION

Despite all these excellent benefits, you need to be aware where you have weaknesses.

From what we have discovered our weaknesses include the following:

1. Inability to accept cash payment per class.

As discussed, allowing students to pay per class is a poor strategic decision for a martial arts business. But if you must, offer a daily rate, so students pay for a day's training rather than a single class.

2. Cost of classes

Unfortunately, not everyone can afford to train at our school. The problem we have is that our expenses are very high due to rent, rates, utilities, and all the other fun of having full-time premises. To keep us in business, we need to charge more than the average church hall operation; otherwise, we would have to close. But we feel we offer excellent value for what we charge when you consider the range of classes available, the facilities, equipment, and the instructor's decades of experience.

3. Timetable (no weekend classes, sometimes classes are a bit late in the evening)

While we offer more classes than the average school, we still have a couple of times in the day when we could offer classes. Early morning classes are proving popular with clients, who want to train first thing and then go to work. Our problem is that we have no shower facilities, so an early morning class seems infeasible.

The other time that we could open is on Sundays. Many people save Sundays for family commitments, but other schools we know have busy Sunday classes. What are your schools USP's and how can you use them in your marketing?

CONCLUSION

So, here we are at the end of the book. I hope you enjoyed it, and got a lot of useful information that you can take into your business to make it more successful

To summarise, in order to build a successful, sustainable martial arts business, you will need to do the following:

1. Decide if opening a martial arts business is really for you.
2. Next decide on the type of business you want (lifestyle vs traditional).
3. Choose the niche market that you want to work with.
4. Define the mission for your business (what do you want it to achieve?).
5. Once you know its mission, create its values and rules.
6. Find the right location for your business (affluent, young families).
7. Find a suitable venue in that location to teach out of (negotiate a rent free period).
8. Use the marketing minimums and more, in order to get a steady stream of prospects calling.
9. Price your classes based on the value that they deliver, not based on what everyone else is charging.
10. Use other revenue streams (equipment sales, seminars, privates) to increase your income.
11. Use Jay Abraham's three ways to grow your business model.
12. Make sure you have excellent customer service.
13. Get to the break-even point.
14. Start making a profit as soon as possible.
15. Reinvest your profits back into your business.
16. Create systems for everything you do in your business.
17. Train people to use the systems so you can work ON your business not IN it.
18. Optimise everything you are doing to make it better.
19. Innovate to stay ahead of your competition and improve your service.
20. Test everything.
21. Educate yourself on best business practices.
22. Get help from a business coach, mentor, or billing company.
23. Schedule plenty of time for rest and renewal (or you will burn out).
24. Remember why you are doing all this.

That last one is important. Sometimes in business it's easy to get caught up in the endless pursuit of profits. Remember why you set your business up. You love sharing martial arts. If you have lost your passion or don't have time to share it with your students, then you may need a little holiday to reconsider your priorities. In the end, as long as you, your family, and your students are happy, then everything should come together nicely.

If you need any help with anything in this book, you can drop me an email at matt@mittmaster.com, and we can run through any points you need to clarify.

Or, if you are interested in getting some coaching from me personally, you can visit my website at matthewchapman.online for details on how I can help you build the business you want. I work specifically with the owners of small martial arts schools that want to grow to a point where their business can support their life and ambitions.

Getting expert help is one of the short-cuts to success, and all successful business people have a team of mentors who act as advisors, role models, confidants, and supporters. Drop me an email if you are ready to take the next step to get more students, more profit, and have more fun.

To your success,

99 WAYS TO GET A STUDENT

99 Ways To Get A Student

Martial art schools are like leaky buckets. As a result of your marketing and advertising new students pour into your bucket. Over time these students start to leak out of the holes in the bucket. Classes get quiet and numbers drop. So what do you do? You pour more students in the top of your bucket.
The cycle begins again and continues year on year.
The secret to building a successful and profitable school is to keep pouring a steady stream of new students into your bucket and to plug the holes in the bucket. If you do this, eventually your bucket overflows and you have a rather wonderful problem. You will have too many students for your school.

The holes in the bucket are any reason why your students are quitting martial arts.

They include:

- Boredom
- Move away from the area
- Work
- Injuries
- Illness
- Family commitments
- Competitors
- Lost interest
- Apathy from the instructor
- Lack of clear goals
- Need has been met

Some of these reasons you are unable to influence, like changes in their work schedule or they move to a different area. But, the great thing is you can plug many of these holes. All of the following holes are under your control:

- **Lack of clear goals** (Set individual goals with each student. Have a compelling syllabus and grading system)
- **Apathy from the instructor** (Care more for your students, keep learning)
- **Boredom** (Teach energetic, entertaining lessons)
- **Injuries** (Make sure students are matched well, monitor sparring carefully, remove risky techniques from syllabus)

However, if you continue losing students through the holes in your bucket, you will need to pour more in the top. If for example, you have one hundred students and you don't do any advertising, eventually that will dwindle down to zero students. It may take 10 months or 10 years. It's an inevitable outcome as everyone quits in the end (even if they just die on the mat, like we plan to).

If you want your school to grow you need to add new members EVERY single month and this is the focus of this book.

To summarise:

A successful martial arts school is based on two core ideas:

1. Adding new students as economically as possible (Sales)
2. Keeping them there for as long as possible (Service)

Sales & Service. Sounds simple, right?

Most martial arts instructors will do bursts of marketing for their school. Then they get busy or lazy and stop. Over time and with natural attrition their student numbers start to drop. They notice a drop in their revenue so they think, "Oh, s**t I'd better do some marketing". They advertise again, for a while, until things start to pick up and then stop again. Many school owners do this and it's the main reasons why their schools don't grow.

As martial arts instructors, we tell our students that inconsistent training leads to inconsistent results. Marketing is no different. It needs to become a daily ritual like eating and washing. You never stop.

Marketing is not a single event it's a process that you keep doing every day you are in business.

Of course, you can create systems and delegate some of the grunt work, but it does need to be done daily for as long as you want to stay in business. There is no other way to achieve consistent results.

The 80/20 principle as it applies to marketing.

80/20 is a concept first discussed by an Italian scientist called Vilfredo Pareto a hundred years ago. **At its core, the theory suggests that 80% of your results will come from 20% of your effort.** Whether this is strictly accurate doesn't really matter but the idea that some things you do will have a bigger effect than others is very important.

This concept applies to the marketing for your school. That is, 80% of your results come from 20% of your marketing activity. Or to put it simply:

80% of your new students come from 20% of your marketing.

Our job as school owners/ instructors is to find out which marketing activities are delivering 80% of your enquiries, and then do more of them. You find this out by keeping accurate statistics on your marketing activities. For example, when you create a new flyer include a code on it that allows you to find out how many enquiries it gets. When someone brings in the flyer or quotes the code you can track it. **This will tell you how cost effective your advertising is.** Do this for any marketing tactic you use: Facebook posts, referral schemes, flyers or school demos.

Once you have worked out your highest performing marketing tactics you can focus on the 20% that get you 80% of your students.

The 20% for my school is from dominating the first page of Google and referral systems. Just these two marketing activities generate 80% of my new students. For you, it may be different and that's why you need to test what will work for you. I am certain that well-designed websites that dominate Google, social media adverts and referrals are the top performers in the majority of martial arts schools, but you never know. You might do amazing demos that have people signing up on the spot. **You've got to track and test different marketing tools to see what works best for you.**

To quote Bruce Lee (As everyone does in every martial arts book)

> ***"Research your own experience"***

What works great for me, may not work for you. Test, track and measure to see what works best for you and your school.

In this book we will look at 99 ways that I have personally used, to attract and sign up new students. **Initially, you will want to focus on the tactics that have the biggest return for the least money invested.** For me and the majority of schools I've interviewed, the big three currently are:

- **Dominating** the first page of Google for your key search terms.
- **Targeted social media marketin**g in your local community.
- **Referral schemes** so students refer their friends and family at
- every opportunity.

Once you have tested these key marketing activities and created systems to implement and automate them, you can look to see if any other of the marketing tactics will outperform them.

In the UK, the average martial arts school has between 20 and 50 members at any one time. I class these schools as "small schools". There is nothing wrong with having a small school if your goal is to run and maintain a small school. However, if you want a larger school then you will need to do lots of cost effective marketing.

You will want to apply the 80/20 principle and discover which marketing methods bring you the most enquiries for the least amount of time, money and energy.

I, for example, don't do demos at my school. The effort it takes to train a demo team, book events and organise students is not practical for me. I'd rather focus on other marketing activities that are less energy intensive, but that's just me. You need to find your core marketing activities that are not only economically effective but also worth your time and energy. This is a personal choice.

How to use this book

I would read this book once, taking notes as you go. At the end of the book are a summary and action plan. Complete the action plan and you will have a comprehensive marketing plan for the following weeks, months and year.

Work your plan, track everything and test new ideas to see if they outperform your best marketing techniques. Once you've read the book and created your marketing plan you can dip in and out of the book as needed. Skim through it and find a new marketing idea that you like the look of and try it out. Keep accurate statistics on how it performs against your controls and if it works better than what you are doing currently make it the new control that you try to beat.

I've included 99 ways to get a new student because as respected marketer Dan Kennedy once said:

"I don't know one way to get sixty customers, but I do know sixty ways to get one customer"

It would be great if I could give you just one way to get a hundred students but unfortunately, marketing rarely works like this. Usually, it's a combination of many advertising techniques working together in unison that gets the prospect to pick up the phone and call.

People these days are very sales resistant and like to have lots of information before they make a decision. **Our job as martial arts instructors is to create a marketing mix that establishes us as the pre-eminent health and fitness professional in our local area.**
This is achieved by using a wide range of marketing activities to bring your school to the front of people's minds when they are ready to begin martial arts training.

Anyway, enough theory.

Let's get to the meat and potatoes. 99 Ways To Get A Student...

1. Referrals

Most of my new students are referrals from existing students. At my school, out of every 100 new members, at least 60 of them come from referrals. Why do we want referral students? Because they are easier to sign up. Their friend has done all the "sales" work for you.

They tell their friend:

"My new kickboxing class is so cool. I'm losing weight and I'm having fun. The students are so friendly and the instructors are so welcoming. You should come with me sometime."

Their friend has just been sold. You don't have to prove anything to them, you just need to ensure they have a good time in their trial class and they will join up. Their friend has done all the persuasion for you and because they know and trust their friend they are more likely to take action and come for a trial.

You can preach to someone for hours about the benefits of martial arts, but if they don't know or like you, they won't believe you. But, if their friend tells them it's fantastic, they are convinced, no questions asked.

In this case, all you need to do as an instructor is be welcoming, make sure they feel at ease and teach a great class. Their friend has already educated them about all the benefits of training. Your job is to confirm to them that they have made the right choice. **For this reason, referrals are far easier to convert into members, they are less price sensitive and will spend more money when they do join.** And, they are also more likely to refer your school to other people, as that's how they were introduced.

This is why referrals are vital to your business. **The most successful schools have formal referral programs in place, where they strategically encourage referrals every month.** Small schools don't have a referral program in place. They just leave it up to their students to take the lead and refer new prospects voluntarily.

Most people, however, need to be encouraged to give referrals. People are busy or they may just forget to mention their martial arts training to their close circle. As a school owner, it's your responsibility to investigate various ways to get your students to refer new members.

Some of my most successful referral methods include:

Offer a tangible reward for a referral that joins your academy. This could be cash, vouchers or a physical piece of equipment. Before you offer a reward you will need to figure out how much you can afford to invest to get a new student. Obviously, you don't want to offer £100 for a new student referral if they are only going to stay with you a short time, as you won't be able to recoup the marketing investment.

It's important to work out what you can afford to pay to get a new student referral. If your offer is too large it will eat into your profits, if it's too small it won't motivate people to take action. Once again you will need to test to see which reward works best for you and how it compares to your other marketing activities. Ideally, you will want to cover the costs of the referral as soon as the new person joins your school.

Currently, at my school, we offer a £25 equipment voucher and a hug (Yes, an actual physical hug) for a referral who joins. See pic below:

Weirdly, I'm usually asked for the hug first. (Not sure what this says about society.) Please be aware, this is only for a referral that joins my school after their free trial class.

You could also offer a reduction on your students training fees when their friend signs up. I am, however, reluctant to do this, as knocking 10% off a student's training fees adds up to quite a lot over a period of 3 - 5 years. But of course you are not me, you will need to test and see what works for you.

It is also acceptable to just ask your students for referrals. At the end of a class you could say:

"Thank you for coming today, if you enjoyed the class let your friends and family know, we'd appreciate it."

It's simple, direct, and it works.

At my school, we give every new person that joins two VIP passes to give to their friends and family. This business card sized VIP pass gets their friend two weeks free training. It's a convenient size and is printed on high-quality card. Make sure it looks and feels like it has value. See below:
Cheap paper cards won't cut it here. It has to look and feel professional. This means new students can actually give their friends something physical when they speak to them about their great experience at your school.

Other schools I've visited encourage referrals by hanging a large sign on their wall saying:

"The best compliment you can pay your instructors is to refer your friends and family".

This acts as a continuous reminder to your students when they visit your school, to be actively thinking about referrals.

Many schools host a 'bring a buddy day'. This is a set day, for example, the first Monday of every month, when your students can invite guests to the school to train with them in class. If you run this event regularly it will help to get your students thinking about referrals. At the end of class say;

"Hey kids, don't forget next Monday is bring a buddy day, please bring a friend who doesn't train with you to class".

It will start to build momentum when it becomes a regular occurrence and form part of your marketing plan. Ensure this buddy class is fun and energetic. Make certain you have your marketing materials and special offers ready so you can pass them to the parents of the new kids after the session.

So, there you have eight different referral methods which you can try in your school next week. Try them all and see which one outperforms the rest. Use the best ones and tweak them to see if you can improve their effectiveness.

These examples are by no means exclusive, there are many other ways to get referrals. Marketing genius, Jay Abraham, has come up with 94 ways of getting a referral. Make sure you find out about a few of his methods as well. **When it comes to referrals the key is to be consistent and constantly remind people: Here are some ways to do this:**

• Invite new trials to bring a friend with them to their first lesson.
• Ask people if they know anyone else who would benefit from training when they sign up for a class.
• Put signs up in your school politely asking for referrals.
• Ask students at the end of the class to refer new members.
• Do regular referral drives (bring a buddy day, bring a sibling day, parent's class etc.).

Keep asking for referrals. I promise it will get easier and become a core part of your marking plan. Some referral tactics will work better than others. Some that work for you won't work for me and vice versa. It's important that you test these methods for yourself.

Remember, referred students are the best type of prospect. **They are similar to your current students, they will join more easily, stay longer, spend more money and refer other people to your school.**

PLUS they are frequently **FREE**.

Having a systematised referral program is, therefore, essential if you want to create a successful and profitable school. Go set one up now!

2. A Converting Website

The next big thing to tackle, after referrals, is creating a converting website. Your website design needs to focus on converting people, looking for martial arts classes on Google, into prospects who come in for a trial and then sign up as members. And then hopefully stay for life!

Unfortunately many martial art instructors' websites are vanity sites. That is, the website is focused on stroking the instructor's ego. There will be a picture of the instructor wearing his eight title belts, boasting about what he has done and who he has beat to get there. For a new person looking to start martial arts, none of this really matters to them. **It doesn't show them any of the benefits of martial arts training, and it doesn't sell the school.**

It's important to remove your ego from your website and focus on the benefits of martial arts for new students. Make all the content focused on how you can help the prospect achieve their goals (fitness, weight loss, confidence, self-defence, competition etc.).

Next, your website needs to have a clean, clear structure and be easy to navigate. Your website should contain essential information, but leave room for questions in the prospects mind. Why? Because ultimately we want them to contact us. Then we can sell our school to them, without them making decisions based on the information on your website.

We want them to call or email and ask "Do you do this?" or "How much do you charge?" **If there is too much information on your site they may well make the "buying" decision without ever making contact with the school. We want to avoid this.** So don't fill every page with information. Make the prospect get in contact to find out what they really need to know.

Keep your website simple.

I have tested both simple and complex designs and my results show that simple, clear and concise works best. I used to have a very busy website that featured too much "stuff" (the history of our school and instructors, our philosophy, our training ethics and everything about our martial arts). This was intimidating to prospective members. It was overwhelming them. They got lost in it all and didn't get in contact. Now my websites are simpler, more focused and easier to navigate. Remove a lot of the junk and "extra stuff" you have on your website, it's distracting and pointless. Here's a rule to follow:

If it doesn't help sell your school and the lessons, remove it!

Create multiple style specific sites

I currently have eight websites for my school. It used to be commonplace to have one website with all of your school's information in one place. However, what is working better for me (and a lot of other school owners I've interviewed), is to create multiple micro sites. **Microsites are small, two to four-page websites focused on a particular keyword/s for which you want to rank highly on Google.**

I currently have a kickboxing only website, a MMA only website, a BJJ website, our main academy website and a few others. I choose to have separate sites that focus on each of the styles we offer at my school. The reason this works is because they all lead back to the same place, me. I am placing my school's name and info all over the web for Google to find. All of my websites rank on the first page of Google and all of the other search engines because they are relevant.

Try to think what someone would type into Google when they are searching for martial arts classes. It would be something along the lines of: "kickboxing near me", "kickboxing classes in (your town)", karate lessons in (your town)" etc. Each microsite needs to contain the search terms that someone would type into Google.

For example a website for MMA in Bletchley, should feature "We teach MMA in Bletchley", "We are the best club in Bletchley for Mixed Martial Arts" or "We teach MMA to the local community in Bletchley". All the information on the site is focused on MMA and Bletchley.

That's exactly what I do on my micro sites. I create small specific sites for each of the styles or classes I teach. If you teach one style you could have separate websites for your kid's classes, adult classes, and private lessons. Getting your keywords on your various micro sites (in the right places: in your titles, meta descriptions and sales copy) should lead to Google domination.

Google Domination means that you own the majority of listings on the first page of Google in your local area, for your key search terms.

If you look at the image below. I own (or are listed on) 8 of the 10 websites shown on the first page of google for the search term "Kickboxing Loughton".

This means 8 times out of 10 anyone searching for kickboxing classes in Loughton is going to click on one of my websites. **When you get this (and it's not that hard to do, just basic SEO techniques) it means you get a steady stream of interested enquiries every week for FREE.**

WordPress or Template Website Builders?

Previously, I built my sites using WordPress. WordPress is a popular website creation platform. It's very powerful, easy to modify and maintain. However, I started to have a lot of security issues with WordPress, resulting in our websites redirecting to XXX adult sites. Not ideal when someone is searching for kids martial arts classes!

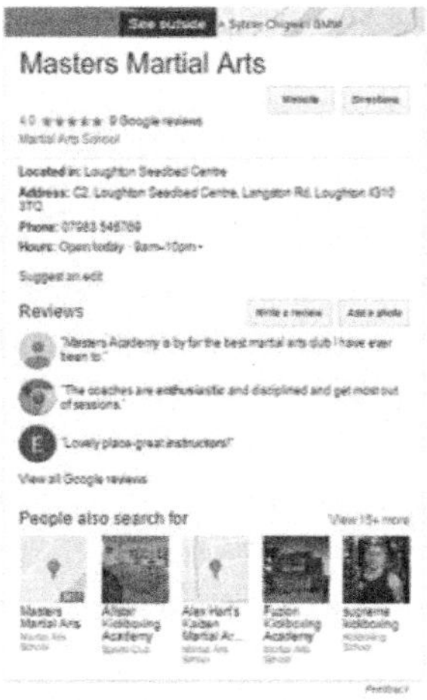

After a couple of weeks of problems, I decided to ditch WordPress in favour of a template website builder called WIX. WIX is much simpler to use for non-techies and puts you in control of the design and layout of your website. **It has a drag and drop builder which means that an untrained person (read: most martial arts school owners) are able to build a clean and simple website within a day.**

WordPress is a far more powerful platform but it does take some time and training to use correctly. If you have the time and inclination it's best to use WordPress for your main school's site. WIX, (www.wix.com,) you can pretty much use immediately with no training.

WIX makes it really easy to build your own microsites with zero technical skills. You can use any of their pre-installed templates (templates are how your website will look), which will give you your basic website style and function. I commonly use a template called 'Boxing Club' which works well for martial arts themed websites. I was able to build my MMA Loughton website (www.mmaloughton.co.uk) in a day and 48 hours later it was number one on Google for the search "MMA Loughton". So, they are serious about their SEO (search engine optimisation) too.

I would recommend that you try WIX to create your micro sites. **By building your own websites it puts you in control and allows you to make changes easily.** It can be very frustrating to wait weeks to get a simple change on your website done by a "professional". Plus you won't get ripped off by dodgy designers trying to charge you £2000 for a basic website that's actually worth only £300.

When building your micro sites think about how they will be found when being searched on Google. Think of keywords prospects might use such as: "self-defence training", "kickboxing classes", "BJJ lessons" or "MMA training near me". You will want to use these keywords in your page titles, descriptions and sales copy. This helps Google rank your website.

What shall I put on my website?

If you are not sure what to feature on your website you can visit some of mine and copy what I've done:

www.mastersacademy.co.uk
www.mmaloughton.co.uk
www.kickboxingloughton.co.uk

At the top right of every page is my school's contact information. That should be in the same place on every page. Visitors shouldn't need to click back through pages to find out how to contact you. Keeping your contact information consistent on every page will ensure that your potential students will know where to find it when they are ready to ask questions.

I have kept my websites simple, the bare bones, without too much information. **They are focused on the benefits of training at my school.** I include some enticing offers to encourage visitors to sign up for information, request a callback or get in contact.

Include an irresistible offer on your homepage

An irresistible offer could be;

"Free trial, Free gloves & Free Fitness Assessment"

Or any variation you want to try. It needs to be an offer that they would be mad not to take you up on. Think of your own and test it. **Also, test if it's cost effective for you.** There is no point in giving away a pair of £50 gloves if you don't make that money back immediately when they join.

Have numerous calls to action

It's also important you have 'calls to action' to encourage the visitor to take action immediately and not think "I'll come back to that tomorrow" (because they never do).

Two simple ways to do this is to have a time sensitive offer (i.e. this offer expires on XYZ date) or have limited numbers available (i.e. only 10 spaces left). **These scarcity tactics encourage people to take action in case they miss out.** People are more motivated to take action if they feel like they are missing out on something. This is very important.

Offer paid trials

I have recently changed the way I sell my MMA classes as I was getting a lot of time wasters. You know, the people who want to be the next Conor McGregor but, not do the 10 years training. **To solve this problem I ditched our free trial and now offer a six-week paid beginners course.** I've tested it and it works better for me than the free trial.

Since we have moved to the six-week course we have had more quality enquiries and they pay in advance (which is better). It's also eliminated most of the timewasters, as they aren't willing to pay for a course.

This reminds me of an important point. One of the key signs of a quality client is;

"Do they have the money to pay for the training?"

By only offering paid beginners courses prospects answer this question because they have to pay to get on the course. You can also offer them some bonuses to encourage them to sign up. I give them a free pair of MMA gloves and a copy of the book I wrote about MMA.

This serves two purposes: It gives them a new set of gloves to get them started and also makes them think...

"Wow, he has written a book, he must know what he's doing".

This increases the value of the course and instills the belief that they have chosen the right school because the instructor is an "expert". Anyone who writes a book is automatically considered an expert by most people. More on this later.

3. SEO

Let's talk a bit more about website SEO (search engine optimisation). **SEO is about getting your websites on the first page of Google naturally (that is without paying to be there)**. Of course, there are numerous ways to achieve this. The first thing to consider is the websites URL (its www. address). What is your current website URL or domain name?

If your URL doesn't include your style and the town you teach in, it won't be as searchable. The majority of people looking for a martial arts class will type the martial arts style they are looking for and their local town into a search engine (usually Google). **It, therefore, makes sense that your website URL should include both your style and your local town.** But, many martial arts schools don't do this. They usually use the chief instructor's name as the URL. But no one is searching for your name, they are looking for martial arts in their local area.

So, your first step is to buy a domain address that includes your style and location. For example, I own www.mmaloughton.co.uk. You will want to do the same for all your niche websites. This helps Google find your website whenever someone searches for your style and your town.

Use GoDaddy: https://uk.godaddy.com/ to buy your domain names.

Using keywords

If you look at my MMA Loughton site, the keywords *MMA Loughton, Loughton MMA, MMA classes in Loughton*, and we teach *MMA classes in Loughton* are featured multiple times in the titles, descriptions and sales copy.

Google, therefore, understands that because the keywords MMA & Loughton are mentioned repeatedly throughout the site that this page would be good to show someone searching for "MMA classes in Loughton". However, make sure you don't overdo using keywords. Your website still needs to read well and make sense to a real person or Google will penalize you. DO NOT stuff your keywords in at every opportunity.

If you use keywords effectively and your website is well designed AND people engage with it Google will shoot it to the top of their rankings. If you do this with several niche websites you will start to dominate Google in your local area.

Other factors to consider with SEO are how long your website keeps the visitor's attention? Do people go to your website and leave immediately because it's confusing or do they get in contact? Does it have a good reputation and sit in the right space on the internet? Does it have lots of links from other websites pointing back to it? All these things affect your ranking on Google.

The age of your website also affects how well it will rank. My Masters Academy website is very old and it sits comfortably at the top of Google, but, as I mentioned earlier, my MMA Loughton microsite shot straight to the top of Google within 48 hours. This means that if the content is relevant, specific and interesting to people then Google is more likely to rank it highly.

There are over 200 factors that effect where your website shows up on Google. I've briefly covered a few, the full list is obviously way beyond this book. Do a little research and you will find the key factors that will help your martial arts school rank highly on Google.

4. Website Usability

Test how easy it is to use your website by asking non-martial arts friends to visit it and have a look around. Then ask them for feedback on how they found the experience. Tell them to be brutally honest.

Here are some good starter questions:

Was the website easy to use?
Was it fun to use?
Did you find all the information you wanted?
Did you ever feel lost or confused?
What did you like?
What didn't you like?

This will give you valuable information about how to best set up your website from a user's perspective. If your website is confusing or frustrating you will be losing many prospects because they will click away before you can communicate the value of martial arts training.

Also, ask your friend to search for specific things on your website such as "information about kid's classes" or "the school's location". Make sure you note how easily and quickly they found the information. This will help you improve your website and find out how usable it is for your customers.

If more than one of your "test pilots" are having the same problem chances are there is something you need to change to make your website more user-friendly. Don't get precious about your website. It's only a tool to help you get more students. You should be willing to change it in an instant if it can be improved.

Last time I had a friend review my website, she made a list of 50 issues that were causing her problems. Getting your website right for the user is vital because if a prospect gets frustrated they will click away and you will never hear from them again.

5. SMO (Social Media Optimisation)

Search Engine Optimisation (SEO) is very important right now, but times are changing and SMO (Social Media Optimisation) is becoming more relevant. **People are no longer only using Google to search for information. They are now using social media too.** Twenty years ago you found out about martial arts via a flyer or in the yellow pages (remember that?). Five years ago you found the same information using Google. Now social media has become the new search tool.

I often see people posting a question on Facebook, asking if anyone knows of, or can recommend local martial arts classes. **Instead of going to Google to find out about local martial arts classes themselves, many people are seeking recommendations from their social media "friends".** This will become more common until it becomes the primary way people search for local information (within 5 years in my opinion).

You, as a local business owner, need to be on social media and known as the martial arts "expert" in your town. Once you gain the status as THE local "martial arts guy/girl", people will automatically mention your school and how good it is.

Speaking of social media it's important to have a social media strategy. You can't just post occasional pictures of your gradings and seminars.

In order to own your local area on social media, you will need to post training tips, fitness advice, nutrition plans, self-defence techniques and lots of information to support your student's training. **You need to do this DAILY in order to build a strong social media presence in your local area.**
Becoming well known on social media takes time, effort and consistency, but it's becoming increasingly important for the school owner. Commit to building your social media presence by sharing valuable information with students and the local community daily!

6. Website load speed

If your website takes longer than three seconds to load, 30-40% of people will click away. People are impatient now. They want the information NOW! Ensure you are using internet friendly media so that your website loads faster. Reducing your photos to 72 dpi is a good place to start. You will crush the file size but still retain the correct quality for a screen or mobile device. I would also advise that you don't use auto-play videos because what happens in the background slows down your website.

Use Google webmaster tools to check how fast your website loads and then follow any advice it gives to speed it up. Speed matters with today's short attention span.

7. Is your website mobile friendly?

Is your website mobile friendly? That is, does it look good and work on a smartphone screen? **Approximately 60-70% of your prospects will be visiting your website via their mobile phone, so your website needs to look and work well on mobile devices.** In addition, if your website hasn't been optimised for mobile Google won't rank it.

If your website is made on WordPress there are many themes, plugins, and converters out there that ensure this happens smoothly. WIX will do all this for you automatically and you can edit your mobile website. This helps you see exactly how it will look on a smartphone before you publish it.

You can visit: https://www.google.co.uk/webmasters/tools/mobile-friendly/ to see if your website is mobile compatible. If it's not, fix it immediately.

8. Write a blog

Do you want your website to have a blog? If you enjoy writing a blog is a great place for you to publish your work. Or, like me, you might just want to use your blog as a way to increase your keyword count and make your website more visible to Google. I'm not that worried about people reading my articles. **I have a blog for Google to search and then rank me for certain keywords**.

Your blog posts can also be a simple way to draw people from social media and drive them to your website. Include the beginning of a blog post on your social media page and ask people to click to your website to read the full article. This drives traffic to your website and helps its ranking. For example, you could do a post on Facebook about bullying and link it to the full article on your website.

9. Remarketing

I'm sure you've had the experience where you've left a website and then been followed around the net by ads for the same website. That's remarketing in action. Remarketing is an advanced internet marketing technique, which works by tracking the websites you visit and then showing you ads for the same websites on Facebook or Google.

It was developed because 60 - 80% of people who visit your website don't do what you want them to do. As school owners the primary thing we want prospects to do is to get in contact: Either sign up for classes, send you an email or give you a call. **Remarketing gives you a second opportunity to speak to these people,**

by showing them an advert after they have left your website, in the hope that they will get in contact.

You have to pay for remarketing and it is a level up from the normal adverts or boosted posts you might use on Facebook. Make sure you get some training or ask for help from a social media professional before you spend any money. But remarketing has been proven to work time and time again.

10. Facebook live

Facebook live is a great tool for getting yourself known locally on social media. Basically, it allows you to film video from your phone and broadcast it live on your Facebook page. You may want to set a time each week to film live tips and training techniques for your students, or try streaming some of your classes and invite people to try out a free session. Include a time sensitive irresistible offer during the video to tempt people to get in contact.

You could also invite your local community to watch a Facebook live event as you share "Self Defence Safety Tips For Kids", for example. Advertise this in advance on Facebook to encourage your local community to tune in. Invite everyone down to your school for a FREE trial at the end of the presentation (use a special code to track responses).

11. Facebook private groups

Private groups are very useful if you want to market to your current students. You could have a whole host of private groups for your school: one for black belts, one for parents, a women's only group etc. This allows you to speak and market directly to a specific group of students. For example, if you have a parents Facebook group you could remind them of your "bring a buddy day" or let them know about you latest offers for family memberships. Groups help you boost student retention by creating a community online. Use groups to share useful information targeted to specific needs.

Just be aware of how time-consuming it can be to manage all of those groups. You will need to schedule time to do this.

Other social media channels

You could also consider using other social media channels, For example, my school has a twitter account. To save time I have set up my Facebook page to post directly to Twitter whenever I publish new content on Facebook. So I kill two birds with one stone. This gets my schools info out there for more people to find.

Instagram, (owned by Facebook), is another great platform for sharing

martial arts content. Instagram is focused on photos and short videos and all the content is searchable via hashtags (# or keywords). #Hashtags are widely used on Social Media and important for getting your content seen, especially if you make your post topical.

It's important to keep an eye on the new emerging social media platforms. New trends are continually evolving and you will get left behind if you don't keep up. For example, many younger students (under 20) no longer use Facebook, as they consider it too old. If you want to market to this younger demographic you need to go where they are (which is Snapchat).

12. Local Facebook groups

I post in the 'Loughton Mums' group every Monday. I am not a mum, I'm a dad. But, I advertise my women's only kickboxing and kids kickboxing classes there. I use a specific advert, to reach this specific target audience.

It's easy to search for local groups on Facebook and request to join them. Search for buying and selling groups, services groups, fitness groups, and mums and kids groups. Join them and post useful information there. **Add value and help people. Share useful information specific to the group you are posting into.** Posting tips about how kickboxing helps lose baby weight will work really well in a mums group for example.

Also, make sure that you are posting from your school's Facebook page. This ensures that interested prospects will find your school's Facebook page and information. If you post from your personal page they will click through and likely see some pictures of you on holiday or worse the hangover pictures. Not ideal for your business brand.

Posting to Facebook groups is part of my weekly online marketing schedule. **Two to three times a week I will post to local groups with content containing offers, testimonials, weight loss successes or short video clips promoting our classes.** It's a simple idea, doesn't cost any money and can create a lot of attention for your school.

13. Facebook competitions

Currently, Facebook will let you run 'like and share' competitions. I'm not sure how much longer this will continue, but it's still possible. Here's how you do it, create an attractive image to do with your martial arts classes and post it with the following text:

"Like and Share this picture to be in with a chance of winning XYZ".

Or try:

"Like and Share this picture to win two weeks free classes".

The cost to you is zero and the potential local audience is large.

14. Facebook Ads (or any paid ads platform)

Facebook (and all ad platforms) are constantly evolving. Therefore, any specific advice I give you now may be different or obsolete within a few months. For this reason, I'm not going to cover how to specifically run ad campaigns on Facebook but rather give you some basic paid ad marketing principles which will work whether you use Facebook ads, Google ads, Tik Tok ads or whatever comes next

Principle 1: Choose the right campaign objective

All ad platforms allow you to choose an objective for your campaigns. For the majority of martial arts schools, you'll want to focus on Lead Capture campaigns. Lead capture campaigns will capture both your prospects email and telephone number. That means you will have three ways to contact your leads (email, phone call, text). You can also direct them to your website after they have given you their details (which means you can track them with the Facebook pixel as well)
Lead form (or lead capture campaigns) get you the most customer data for your ad spend so should be the focus of your paid ad strategy. But feel free to test other campaign objectives like messaging or traffic to website to see how they perform when compared to a lead form ad.

Principle 2: Choose the right audience

All ad platforms allow you choose a specific audience to show your ads to. For local business marketing this is relatively easy as you only want to include people who are within travelling distance of your school. There's no point in advertising to get members from 200 miles away. Work out a radius around your school where 80% of your students live and market there.

You can also target specific demographics within that local audience. For example, if you are launching a new women's only class it would make sense to show your ad to "women only"

Or perhaps you are opening a new kid's class for children aged 7-11. Well on a lot of ad platforms you can target local parents with kids aged 7-11. You can't get any more targeted than that!

My advice is to explore all the targeting options available to you and see what works best.

Principle 3: Make your creative POP

The creative is what you use to persuade your prospect to stop scrolling and start reading your ad. Creative usually describes the images or video you use in your ads. The whole goal of creative to stop your prospect in their tracks and make them think "wow, this is for me". Once you do that, they will read your headline and the rest of your ad, but if you cannot stop them scrolling no one will see you ad. For this reason, your creative needs to be high quality and "pop out" of the feed. Bright images, contrasting colours, smiling faces, movement, bold text and emotion all help your creative to pop

One of the best resources you can use to find ideas for creative (and copy) is Facebook ads library. And that's exactly what it sounds like. It's a library of all current running Facebook ads. Just enter your country and the keyword "martial arts" and you'll see every Facebook ad that martial arts schools are running in your country. As you scroll through the ads see which ones pop off the page and attract your eye. Use similar colours, images and ideas from these ads in your own ads. DON'T copy other instructors' ads and copy. That's bad form, just use their ads for inspiration to create your own.

Principle 4: Write engaging copy

Copy are the words on the ad that persuade a prospect to take action. Most instructors struggle with writing copy which is understandable as they are not copy writers. It's good when you start writing copy to use simple formulas that help structure your work. For most martial arts schools I've worked with the following formula performs well when creating ads

Call Out

Call out your target audience. For example: "Parents of kids aged 7-11 in Bristol"

Problem

Talk to the target person about problems they may be experiencing. For example:

"Are your kids spending too much time on their devices? Are they getting enough exercise? Are the struggling to cope with peer pressure at school?"

Solution

At XYZ martial arts school our classes help get children out of their rooms and around other positive kids all working towards improving their health, mindset &

fitness

Testimonial

But don't take our word for it, here's what Sarah said about her child's experience at our schools

Add Short Testimonial from Sarah

Offer

We are offering 10 Bristol based children the opportunity to try out our fun martial arts classes

Response

To book your child into out FREE one week trial please click the button below and ontor your details, we will be in touch within the hour to get them started on their martial arts journey

A great copywriter called Ray Edwards invented this copy formula. Check out his book "How to Write Copy That Sells" to learn his complete system. It's an easy read and will massively improve your ability to write persuasively. Highly recommended.

With copy, the more you write, the better you get, so keep practising.

Principle 5: Have a GREAT offer

Most martial arts schools use some variation of the FREE trial class to attract prospects. The FREE trial class still works but it's so BOOOORING.
Try to create a more interesting and engaging offers and test them to see how they perform. When you test 10-20 offers, you'll eventually hit on the one offer that outperforms all the rest, but you'll have to experiment to get there

A great offer includes the following 12 elements

1. Its unique (so can't be compared to other martial arts schools offers)
2. It's got a interesting name (so people remember it)
3. It is targeted at one specific person or group (such as parents of kids aged 7-11)
4. It has one clear promise or result
5. It is presented as a stack (separate all the elements of the offer and present them as a bundle)

6. The stack has visuals & videos (people have no imagination so show them exactly what they are getting)

7. It includes bonuses that overcome objections (like a guide to deal with bullying that the parents can read)

8. It is scarce (only 10 spaces available)

9. It is urgent (and this offer ends on....)

10. It includes a guarantee

11. It includes social proof (testimonials & reviews)

12. It has a clear call to action (what do they need to do next)

Try to combine as many of these elements as possible when creating your own offers. The more elements you include the stronger your offer will be.

Principle 6: Test, Test, Test

Its very rare to have an ad campaign work perfectly the first time around. You have to be willing to test different objectives, offers, creative and copy to find a wining campaign. Most instructors try a Facebook ad once, it doesn't work as well they wanted, and they pronounce "Facebook ads don't work"
You have to willing to spend a bit and test a lot to find your unique winning ad formula.

- First you should test the campaign objectives
- Then you should test different creative
- Then you should test different versions of your copy
- Then you should test different offers

Luckily with many ad platforms it's easy to test these elements against each other quickly but it's beyond this book to show you how. Speak to a trained Facebook ads expert to learn how to test different ad elements quickly.

Principle 7: Pay attention to your metrics

When running paid ads its important to pay attention to the results you are getting. You should be able to work out quickly whether an ad is working based on the metrics in your ad dashboard. You'll want to keep an eye on your cost per result, your link click through rate, frequency & CPM (cost per 1000 impressions)

If you are not sure what these metrics mean, get onto your ads platform training library or go to YouTube to learn more. You shouldn't really be running ads if you don't know how to measure what's working and that requires an understanding of the metrics listed above.

Principle 8: Understand retargeting

Retargeting is advertising to prospects who have already interreacted with your business. For example, if someone sees your Facebook ad and goes to your website after filling out a lead form you can retarget them with ads because they....

a. Interacted with your ad

b. Went to your website

This means that you can follow up with them by showing them other content such as testimonial videos, class promos or special offers

Retargeting (or remarketing as its sometimes known) is all about follow up. If a prospect doesn't become a paid member after seeing your first ad you keep following up with them via phone, email, text AND using paid ads to persuade them to become a member.

Retargeting ads are usually some the most cost-effective ads you can run

Those are my principles of paid marketing. Those principles work whether you are using Facebook, Google ads, Tik Tok ads or any other paid platform. My advice is to have a marketing budget for experiments that you use each month to test new ideas. For example, you could budget £300 a month for paid ads experiments and don't worry about your initial results as you are learning.

The more you learn about digital ads for local business the better your results will get so spend some time getting educated about digital marketing. All platforms have online training about how to run ads on their platform so that's a great place to start. I'd also recommend Einstein Marketer's free marketing blog. It's packed full of useful information you can use to improve your digital marketing skills.

15. Timing Facebook posts

If you are not boosting your posts, (or don't yet have the budget to do so), you need to time your Facebook posts for maximum reach. I used to post at 11:00pm when I got home from teaching, and couldn't figure out why no one was engaging with my posts. The reason is the only people awake at that time were other martial arts instructors and it's likely they are doing the same thing.

"Regular 9-5 ers" are not normally awake at that time and if they are, they won't be as active on social media. They will be preparing for sleep as they have an early start in the morning. So my posts we poorly timed to attract the type of prospects I wanted.

If you would like to attract office workers there are three prime times to deliver your posts: between 7:00am and 9:00am, (when they are commuting to work), between 11:30am and 1:30pm, (around their lunch break) and finally between 5:00pm and 8:00pm (when they will be on the commute home). These peak times will help you target those that work 9 to 5.

Think about your target audience. If you are trying to target housewives for your women's only classes, then the timings are likely to be after the school run (9-11am) and possibly after kid's bedtime, when they get their life back (7-9pm). Shift workers will also be on social media at different times from both 9 to 5 ers and housewives. The timing of your posts depends on whose attention you are trying to attract.

You can, of course, use Facebook's scheduled post option. This allows you to schedule a date and time that your post will go live. This is a great tool for those that like to be organised and work to a specific posting schedule. It also means it doesn't matter when you are writing the post, you can choose exactly when you would like the post to appear to attract your target customer. Using this tool is a good way to test which times of day are most effective for your business. Find out which times get you the best results.

How to schedule a post

When you are writing a new post on your Facebook page before you publish it you will be able to select the time and date when you would like it to go live. This is great, if, for example, you are not an early riser, but would like to target those early commuters (6am-8am). Your post can be published and go live while you are getting your much-needed sleep.

16. Collaborative content

What if you are running out of ideas for content to use on social media? You can always call on your martial arts friends to create something new for your website or Facebook page. It could be training tips from your instructor or a short video interview with someone you respect. Collaborative work will increase your viewing audience as you will be promoting to your existing students and to your friend's group. These collaborative projects may also lead to other opportunities, (joint seminars for example).

17. Online magazines, forums & blogs

Find out about local online magazines and forums that you may consider using for your advertising. Local crime prevention forums or blogs are great places to start for martial arts instructors. You could feature as a local expert and write weekly or monthly articles which will create back links to your website (great for SEO). All of these things will help you to build your expert profile in your local community and boost your SEO.

18. Viral videos

You could also try to create a viral video. **Videos are shared more than any other type of post.** And fun videos get shared the most! I'm not suggesting that you teach a class butt naked, but I'm sure you can think of a humorous approach or a strong message that will engage your viewers and make them want to share your video.

A viral video is not always something you plan, sometimes your audience will run with something that you never thought would go viral, that's just the luck of the draw.

What's important is that you are producing consistent high-quality content. Content that is liked and shared. Content that is interesting to your target audience and content that has value. This will help to grow your social media reach and presence.

Have you heard of Master Ken and his YouTube channel 'Enter the Dojo"? It's a very funny spoof on martial arts schools. Master Ken has built up a massive following from his videos, many of which have gone viral.
He now charges large amounts of money, to travel around the world, giving spoof seminars at martial arts schools.

That's what viral videos can do for you and your business. Of course, this requires work, time and effort but so does everything of value. If you enjoy using video then this may be a useful marketing tool. If you don't want to do this yourself why not get one of your juniors to create videos for you using their smartphone?

19. School YouTube Channel

Does your school have a YouTube channel? **Google owns YouTube so using it to feature your classes won't do you any harm and may improve your ranking,** (for example, a couple of my YouTube videos appear in the search results above my websites).

Start filming promos, classes, seminars, workshops and testimonials and add them to your school's YouTube channel. It's important to get your video title and description right on YouTube. Your title is what will tempt people to click on your video and then watch your amazing content. **Your title needs to be attention grabbing and relevant for people searching for local martial arts classes.**

Rather than use the title "Paul and John hitting pads" try to include your school name and location such as "Fun Kickboxing Classes at Masters Academy, Loughton. FREE TRIAL". This will be more beneficial to you from an SEO standpoint.

Get really creative and have lots of fun on YouTube. Martial arts content doesn't always need to be serious. Have fun and share your sense of humor in your videos and you will attract students who are similar to you. **Treat your school's YouTube channel like your own private TV channel.** Make it fun, interesting and informative so you reach as many people as possible. Also, make sure you ask students to share your YouTube videos with their friends (it helps if they are in them).

20. Promo video

A promo video should promote what you do, the classes you offer and the benefits of training. It should be a visual representation of what it's like to attend one of your classes. **Many people prefer to watch video over reading text.** If your website is too text-heavy it's likely that a percentage of people will get bored and click away. Include an exciting two-minute promo video on every website you build.

I suggest you create a specific promo for each of the classes you teach, to feature on each of your microsites. Have a kid's promo video, an adult's promo video etc. Ensure that each video shows your members having fun, smiling and enjoying their training.

It's not a good idea to feature students getting choked unconscious, or being kicked in the head, even if that does happen in class. That's more likely to scare people away from your school. **Keep your promo videos positive and safe so you don't intimidate new prospects.**

Make sure you use your own students in your videos as they will share them with everyone they know. Students like to see themselves on film and this will help you generate referrals.

21. Class clips

Try filming 20-30 second mini clips of your classes. These mini video clips are really simple to film and easy to edit using your smartphone. Post class videos to Facebook / YouTube and students they will share it with their social media friends. This may spark up a conversation, for example:

"Oh I didn't know you did kickboxing"
"Yes, it's really fun, would you like to come along with me? You get a free trial?"

"Sure, why not"
BINGO!

You can also film individual students (with their permission or parents permission), asking them to perform their favourite technique or drill. They will, of course, share the video immediately and before you know it, the whole school will want to film their favourite technique (This works great with kids). **It's a very simple idea that can create a lot of free marketing for your school.**

22. Tag your photos

When you post new photos to your school's Facebook page, tag any students in them (or encourage them to tag themselves). Once they have been tagged the picture will show up on their profiles and will be visible to all their Facebook friends. Quite often, students, friends or work colleagues are unaware of their hobbies and will question them to find out more. Your referral action plan should kick in and they will invite their friend down for a free trial class.

23. Google places/ Google My Business

Google My Business allows you to list your local business on Google Maps. You are able to write in detail about your school, upload photos and videos, set your opening times, link to your website, geotag to pinpoint your business on Google maps, create offers and lots more. **If you haven't done this already then I would make it a priority. It only takes a couple of hours and is another tick in the Google box.**

Go to www.google.co.uk/business to register your local business NOW!
Make sure you complete the listing, (don't leave anything out) and then verify your location with Google. **Getting a Google Business listing is essential.**

24. Google AdWords

Google AdWords are paid adverts which place your website above Googles organic searches. Have you seen those "featured" or "sponsored" links when you make a Google search? Those little ads at the top of Google?

If you already use good SEO practices and your websites are showing at the top of Google, don't use Google AdWords. What's the point? You are already ranked at the top of Google, you don't need to also pay to be there. The only reason to pay for ads is if you are not listed at the top.

Then AdWords may get you to the top, but you will have to pay. Also consider, that less than 10% of people click on the ads at the top of Google. Most people scroll down to the natural free listings. **Google AdWords is also very complex when compared to Facebook advertising and, ideally you need training to use it.** Without training, it's very easy to lose money quickly on AdWords. Get some help before using AdWords.

25. Google Alerts

Google alerts are a great way to monitor your school's reputation on the internet. Google Alerts allow you to choose keywords for which you can be "alerted". Google will then send you a daily email each time those keywords have been mentioned anywhere online.

If for example, someone leaves a bad review of your school and you have a Google Alert set up for your school name, you will find out about it immediately. Which means you can then take immediate action rather than finding out about it two weeks later after the damage has been done.

You can also use Google Alerts to track what your competitors are doing online. They might be promoting awesome special offers and you can use this information to create your own counter offer. This helps you stay aware what your competition is doing and allows you to take quick effective action when needed.

To set up the alerts, go to Google and type 'Google Alerts'. Follow the instructions to set up things up and tell Google how often you'd like the summary email sent. I find that a daily email works best so I can see what is happening and respond quickly. **Google Alerts allow you to manage your online reputation, which is obviously good for business.**

26. Online reviews

Reviews on Facebook pages, Google, Yelp, Yahoo etc. count towards your visibility on Google searches. **Google and prospects like to see reviews of your business, as reviews create trust.** If someone else has been there and had a good enough experience to review it, it must be good.

At the end of class ask your students to leave a review on Google or Facebook. Unfortunately, you cannot line them up at the end of a session and use your computer to add all of their reviews in one go. Google will recognise the reviews have come from the same computer and you will get in trouble.

Instead, ask your members on social media to leave a quick review or just click on the stars on your page to help raise the profile of your school. They obviously love your work, otherwise, they wouldn't come every week, so they should do it with pleasure.

27. Testimonials

Talk to your members, ask them why they came to you, why they decided to join your school, and why they stay. **If they are enthusiastic and excited, get them to fill out a short questionnaire on their experience at your school.** Or you could record a video testimonial of how much they enjoy training at your school. This takes less than 2 minutes at the end of class. Use your smartphone and ask them to complete this sentence:

"I love training at "Your School" because......"

If you do this after every class pretty soon you will have many short testimonials you can use on your YouTube channel, Facebook page, and website. People these days often require social proof (in the form of testimonials) before they decide to buy anything. Having 20-30 written and video testimonials will increase your chances of persuading someone to pick up the phone and give you a call.

It is also an opportunity to find out if there are any improvements that need to be made. **This leads to many great ideas about how you can improve your school for its members.**

28. Find the evangelists

In every martial arts school, there will be 10-20% of your members who literally love everything you do, and will tell everyone they meet about how great you are. We have a lovely lady who brings her children to our classes. Her son was a gentle giant and was being bullied at school. Our classes gave him the confidence to stand up for himself and as a consequence, the bullying has stopped.

Over a short period of time, she has referred eight new families to our school **WOW**! She is one of our top referrers and every Christmas we give her a bottle of champagne. It's a small token from us but it sends a big message. **This 20 % of your school (we call them Evangelists) are really important and need extra attention.** They are helping to build your business, so a small token of appreciation is appropriate.

Find out who the evangelists are in your school. Be extra nice, treat them on occasion and they will continue to reward you by talking about your school and referring new members. This takes us back to the 80/20 rule. 20% of your students will be making you 80% of your profit. **Look after these special members because they are earning you extra revenue every time they recommend your school.**

29. Sponsor a local event

Find out all the events that are happening locally, (choose a few that are well attended and are likely to attract your target market). Contact the organizers about becoming a sponsor and get your name, logo and website on their promotional material. The costs can be surprisingly low, plus you will be helping out another organisations work. This builds community bridges.

30. Launch a new product or service

I am launching a new six-week self-defence course soon. This opens up a lot of marketing opportunities specific to this subject. In the past, I used to run a course and no one would know about it, so no one would turn up!

Now, I have a predictable launch process. This is like when a new film is about to be released, there will be a steady stream of video trailers, articles, photos, press releases from the studio. Most of this happens a year before a film gets released to build hype and anticipation.

You should launch your new class or course along those lines. Think about how you can generate excitement 4-6 weeks before your event starts. You could start with a few teaser video clips, share some cool information, do a press release, write blog articles, and more. Creating hype around something new will attract extra attention and create excitement. Try to develop a consistent launch process that generates a lot of enquiries.

31. Find a new niche

There are more than ten martial art schools in my town. I did some research to see which areas my competition are not tapping into. I found that self-defence training was not being taught in my local area. So, I created a six-week course, advertised it locally and attendance has been consistent ever since.

Is there a need for a particular service in your local community that's not being met?

Think about the skills you haven't used in awhile. **How can you take what you've learned and repackage it as a class, course or workshop?** I would recommend that you run a short course. The course can run for six to eight weeks. **Participants must pay for the course in advance, so even if they drop out, you still get paid.** And after the course ends those people that want to continue can sign up for classes or book private lessons.

32. Create Packages

What is a package? **A package is a short course that also includes bonus materials like training equipment, manuals, video downloads and plans.** As there is a lot of extra content included in a package you can charge a premium for them.

From the participant's perspective, they are investing in a complete "package" that will solve a specific problem or teach them a specific skill. They will get all the equipment they need and will have access to course videos, notes, and manuals. After the course, if they want more, it's easy to sell them your private training sessions.

Do you have multiple skills in martial arts? How can you use them? My next package is a kid's nunchaku course. Why? Because kids love nunchucks and I love nunchucks, they are fun. Here's how I plan on breaking it down.

I will set up a four-week Nunchuk course, 45 minutes a session, and charge £30 per child. I anticipate that 20 kids will sign up to the course, and that will bring in £600. I will need to buy some foam nunchucks for the kids to use and keep. After equipment costs, I should earn over £125 per hour. That's a pretty good earner! I will be bringing extra money into my business, without committing to a regular class.

It is important that you set a minimum number to run the course. If you don't you may get one student sign up, and it will be you, them and a lot of spare equipment. Put a sign-up form on the wall of your school six weeks before the event. When you get to 16 attendees, (say the minimum number required is 20), mention at the end of class that you only need four more students to run the course. You will be surprised at how many extra will sign up at that point. If you don't get the minimum number you can decide if you cancel the course.

33. Result based packages

Offer result based packages rather than classes. One of the problems with martial arts training is that it doesn't offer guaranteed results. Result based courses are a great way to attract new students and charge a premium. We run a course called "BTT", (Body Transformation Training). It's a six-week course that focuses on healthy weight loss and body toning. The BTT package is £200 per person for six weeks. Every time we run this course we have 15-20 people sign up.

For this, the clients get martial arts training plus extra boot camp sessions and an 80 page manual on how to eat healthily and improve their diets.

We also set up a private Facebook group to share tips and answer any questions they have during the course. Every week we record their weight and measurements so they get to track their progress over the six weeks. It's not uncommon for a client to lose 5kg of fat during BTT.

This makes it not only "martial arts lessons" you are selling but a "package" with guaranteed results and short-term achievable goals. This means you can charge more than you could just for martial arts classes.

Packages where you offer additional materials and ongoing support are becoming increasingly popular. Can you think of any packages that you could create for your school?

34. Define your difference

How you distinguish yourself from your competitors is very important. **If you don't define how your school is different from your competitors, then prospects will only be able to compare you on price (as they have no other information to base a decision).** How can you distinguish yourself and your school from your competition? What is unique about you? What do you do differently? Why are your classes different from others? What makes your school special?

For example, my friend David Lee runs an MMA school. He is a former UFC fighter, (which is still rare in the UK). There are hundreds of MMA fighters but very few have made it to the UFC. He is also a BJJ black belt and author. If Dave used this information in his marketing he is setting himself apart from his competition. As a prospect, if you are looking for an MMA school you are most likely going to choose the guy who has fought in the UFC.

Think about your skills, about who you are and what you have achieved; how can you use this in your marketing? Remember that prospects have never met you or been to your school, they only know what you tell them on your website. **To you, something could seem insignificant, but in the prospects mind, it could be the defining factor that sets you above the other schools in your area.**

Tom Callos is fond of saying that martial arts instructors think they are telepathic. They know all this great stuff and have helped so many people but they don't use it in their marketing. They just assume everyone can read their mind about the amazing benefits of martial arts training! **You have to tell your story, why you are different, and why people should choose you.**

35. Personalise your business

How can you personalise your business? **First, don't use stock photos on your website. Use real photos of your students.** Your audience will know that they are real and trust them more than cheesy stock photos. Add a photo of you on your website so that when potential members come to your school they see a familiar face. This makes them feel more comfortable.

Add personal touches to your school. Hang pictures of your instructors, have a display cabinet featuring a few trophies (if that's your thing). Add a few of your inspirational quotes to the walls to motivate your students. Make the space reflect your personality as this is attractive to your students.

36. Offer Private Lessons

Private lessons are a great way to generate extra revenue. **As the student is getting your undivided attention the value of your time increases considerably.** Private lessons range from £20-£200+ an hour. And that's not based on the coaches' skill or experience. I know some amazing instructors with 30 years' experience who are only charging £25 an hour. **The price you charge is based on how much you value your time.** Personally, I value my time at £50-100 an hour so won't accept any less than that for one to one instruction. That's just the minimum I have to earn. You may value your time more or less, but don't think that price has anything to do with experience.

Group privates

I have recently begun to change my private lessons to group only sessions. I charge £99 an hour for a group private. That fee is for two to ten people. If there are ten people it's only £10 each. If one person enquires and the fee is too high for them alone, I encourage them to find some friends to do the session with them, making it cheaper and spreading the cost. That way I earn £100 per hour regardless and the group trains together and ultimately get better results.

I did this to reduce the wear and tear on my body because the students train with each other rather than beat me up. **I also noticed small groups tend to be more consistent and motivated because peer pressure makes sure they all turn up to train.** It's easy to cancel a session if it's just you but people don't like to let their friends down, so attendance is more consistent, which is better for them and better for you.

Think about how you set your price. If you need to do privates to increase your cash flow, it's likely that you will have to compete with other instructors in your area. If, like a friend of mine, you don't need to do privates, (mostly because he doesn't like doing them) then charge whatever you like. He charges £100 for one-hour of private instruction. He doesn't really want to do these private sessions, but it's an added bonus when they do come in.

37. Make joining simple

Make it easy for people to join your school. Don't put unnecessary barriers in their way. Here's how it should go:

'Can I join your school?'
'Sure, sign here please.'

Keep it as simple as possible. There is a school near me that only lets people join after they have done an induction that happens once a month. If they miss that induction prospects have to wait a whole month to try again. Madness.

Make joining your school as simple as possible. **If someone would like to join**

your school, let them join immediately. Why would you make a person wait a month to try out your classes? You have to catch prospects whilst they are motivated and excited about starting. Two weeks later they might have joined a different school or lost motivation altogether.

38. Wear your business info

Wear branded kit. It looks professional and you will get asked about it when you are in public places. That's a great opportunity to hand out one of your VIP cards and invite them to a trial session at your school. **So make sure you have VIP passes on you at all times when out wearing your club T-shirt.**

39. Swamp the town

Organise a meet up with 20-30 of your students in your town on a Saturday afternoon. Ask them to wear their uniform to represent your school (or at least your club t-shirt). A large group of people wearing your schools branded uniform attracts attention and will get people talking. It promotes local brand awareness and encourages your members to be social with their training partners which boosts retention. Your students could also hand out flyers. Buy everyone a coffee at the end of the day.

40. Offer a guarantee

Not many martial arts schools offer a guarantee. If you have a guarantee it makes your school very special. I have a triple guarantee at my school. Our first guarantee is:

"Train twice a week for two months. If you don't get fitter we will refund all of your money no questions asked."

They have to train twice a week for eight weeks. If they don't feel fitter they get their money back. **I've had that guarantee at my school for over five years and I haven't been asked for a refund, yet.** What the guarantee does is reduce the risk in the mind of the prospect.

"Oh ok, I could get my money back if I'm not happy".

As mentioned I haven't had to give a refund yet. If someone did ask, I'd just give them their money back. I don't think it's something worth arguing over. Because we all know that after sixteen classes they will feel fitter. They would literally have to come and lie to my face to get their money back. Which no one has, so far!

Add your guarantee to your website and to your Facebook page. It may be one of the deciding factors why someone would choose your school over another. Here's our triple guarantee if you need some inspiration:

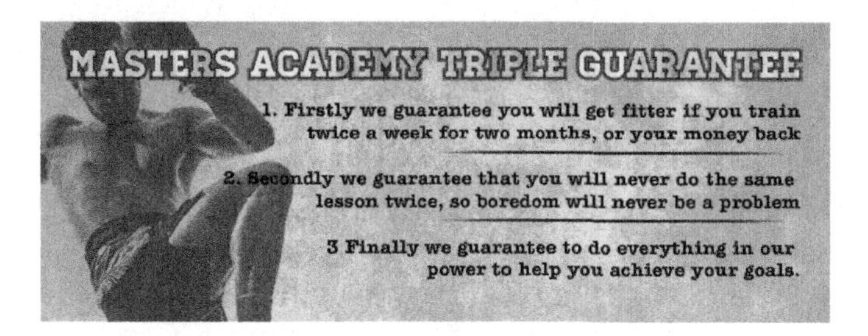

41. Sell Gift Certificates

At Christmas, we sell a lot of gift certificates for equipment and private lessons. The number of people who purchase gift certificates at Christmas is surprisingly high. I guess people can't think of anything else to get someone who trains martial arts. **Plus, private lesson gift certificates are actually a brilliant gift for those that are enthusiastic about their training.** Make sure you advertise your gift certificates in November. Make them look as professional as the ones you'd get on the high street. Check out ours below:

42. Hang a sign/ flag/ banner

If your landlord allows it, hang a flag and an illuminated sign on the outside of your business. The sign obviously shines at night and a flag attracts attention because it moves in the wind. You can also buy freestanding flag poles that look great outside your school and help attract attention. Use whatever external signage you can to attract passing custom.

43. Keep an eye on the calendar for ideas

There are several dates that you should use to promote your business. Key dates are Easter, Summer, Halloween, Christmas and New Years. Even on mother's day, we purchase roses for the children to take home to their mums after class. It's a nice gesture and shows we think about the parents, who selflessly pay for their kid's training.

Valentine kid's camps are also popular. Run a kids training session on valentines night and after class watch a film like Kung Fu Panda. The parents get to go out and have a meal knowing their kids are safe and having fun. If you price it just below local babysitting rates and fill it with thirty kids you'll make a tidy profit. The parents get 3 - 4 hours of peace to themselves. Priceless

At Easter do a referral drive to win a GIANT Easter egg. The person who refers the most students in the four weeks leading up to Easter wins the giant egg. It seems like a silly promotion, but it will get people competitively referring new students to your school.

Summer boot camps and outdoor fitness sessions work well in the warmer months. I used to offer these sessions for free, but people would drop off too quickly. I found if you make people pay for a 6-week course they are more likely to stick to it. Advertise your summer boot camp in late May and add extra value bonuses like nutrition plans to encourage people to sign up.

Be aware, not all public parks allow such activities, especially in London, where the council will want to charge you for using the space, so research the best free spaces in your local town.

At my summer boot camps, we would run to our local nature reserve, spend 20 minutes kicking pads, stretch and run back. Getting out in the fresh air and exercising has to be a good thing. Students love the novelty. It seems crazy but you can charge extra money for the same thing that you do in your school, the only difference is its outside. Give it a catchy name like Body Transformation Boot

Camp and you're onto a winner. Keep an eye on the calendar for ideas.

44. Business Cards

Business cards have been around for over 100 years, but they still work. Do you have some in your wallet or bag right now? I hope so! They're an inexpensive way to promote your business when you are out and about. Talking to someone in the queue for a coffee is a prime example of when these little cards come into play.

Not only will it give you the ability to easily share your school's information it also presents a professional image. I'm sure we've all written our number on the back of a napkin, which is later lost or thrown away. If you create high-quality business cards they are more likely to be kept in someone's wallet or purse for when they are needed.

My favourite type of business cards are 'tent business cards'. These cards are folded in the middle and stand up on their own, in the shape of a tent. These are perfect to leave in cafes and shops as they are eye catching. I keep a batch of these in my wallet at all times and will often leave them around town when I am running errands.

Because, they are double the size of a regular business card, and folded, you can get twice as much information on them. You will be able to include your latest offer and a list of benefits to draw people to your school.

Once a month I would also have some of my teenage members distribute my business cards to different places around my town in exchange for free equipment or training. This makes sure your cards are getting out there in the local community.

45. Demonstrations

Local fetes, events, festivals and carnivals are great opportunities to do a demonstration to promote your school. Always have a part where you allow spectators to come and join in. This makes your demo more interactive and interesting. Have students hand out flyers to the crowd whilst your demo team puts on a show.

If, like me, it's not your thing, use it as an opportunity to encourage your junior students to step up and take the limelight. Get a keen junior black belt to select, organise and train the demo team. Check in now and then to see that they are representing your school as you want and then book them for events from July to September. Make sure you reward demo team members with discounted training fees, extra classes or a special uniform for demo team members only.

46. After school clubs

Many schools run activities after school ends. Although these often don't pay that well, if you are looking to expand your work into schools it's a great way to start. Contact your local schools about after school clubs. Always talk about the benefits of martial arts in terms of discipline, focus, and control. The goal is to upgrade a percentage of the kids into your regular program at your school.

47. School talks

You can offer to give martial arts themed talks in schools. Email the school about coming to present during assembly. You can talk about any of the benefits of martial arts training: fitness, goal setting, persistence, or discipline. Make it active and get the kids to do a few moves. **This is a great way to talk directly to the kids in your local schools and put flyers in their hands to take home.** If you don't like public speaking or kids, I would skip this one. Ha ha

48. School book bags

If you have children at school, you may have noticed them coming home with flyers promoting after school clubs in their book bags. This would also be a good way to advertise your martial arts classes. First, you will need to set up a meeting at the school to deliver your flyers. The school office will then distribute them to the kids in the school. Make sure you mention the benefits of children training martial arts on your flyer and include a special offer.

If you get resistance from the school offer to donate the first month's fees to the school, so not only are their students learning a great new activity, you are raising money for the school.

49. Fundraising flyer

This is a great idea from Master Dave Kovar. If you don't know who Dave Kovar is, go to Google and do some research. **Here's the core idea, contact your local school and tell them you would like to raise money for them.** Tell them you will run a four to six-week martial arts course, exclusively for the students of their school only. **All proceeds from the course will go directly to the school.** Make sure they understand that you don't take any of the fees. In exchange, they will distribute the flyers to the entire school.
Explain to them that your goal is to help the school AND to sign up the students that wish to continue at the end of the course. This is a WIN –WIN for you and the school. And because you are not concerned with making money on the front end you can keep the price low to attract as many prospects as possible. The school ends up making money and at the end of the course you can sign up a percentage of the students to a program at your school. **This idea works REALLY well.** Thank you, Mr. Kovar.

50. Bring a friend to class day

Once a month you can host a 'bring a friend to class day'. Make it easy to remember, for example, the first Monday of every month. Encourage your members to bring a friend to try out a class. This is especially good for kids as they love talking about what they learn at martial arts.

We like to give all of the "guests" a white belt at the end of class so they feel like they've achieved something. In our system, the white belt is the beginner's belt. Everyone at our school will receive a white belt when they start, but the new kids don't know that. They go home so proud and can't wait to show their parents their first belt. **Naturally, they want to join to earn their next belt.**

51. Give Away Motivational Posters

I also used to give away a motivational poster to new students. I use a favourite quote paired with an inspiring image. **People would often put it up where they would see it daily and it would help to motivate them during the inevitable plateaus.** Plus their friends often comment on the posters, which got us a few referrals. Here's one of our motivational posters:

We have a poster for children too (see next page). It reinforces the rules at our academy about listening, paying attention and respecting the academy. I turned this into an A4 size good behaviour contract, which I give to new children when they join my school. It helps them understand that if they behave well, and train hard they will be rewarded come grading time. It also acts as a visual reminder of the black belt behaviours they have committed themselves to. Parents also share this on social media, so it generates referrals for us.

52. Create a beginners guide

There is a lot of information that we'd like to share with new students, but with nearly 400 members it's impossible to do this on a one to one basis. Instead we created a 30-page beginner's guide that contains lots of vital information for new members. It includes:

- What to expect from the classes
- What equipment they will need
- How to get the best from training
- How the belt system works
- How to tie their belt
- Tips for healthy eating

I'm sure that some of these guides end up in the bin, but many will be read by eager students or interested parents. It an opportunity to give them answers to frequently asked questions and to educate them on the numerous benefits of martial arts training. This reduces buyers remorse and sets long-term expectations.

If the guide is for children, you can add a behaviour contract. This is really reassuring for parents, especially mothers who are sometimes a little unsure if they want their kids to learn martial arts. It shows that there is more to your school than kicking and punching. Use the fact you have a FREE beginners guide in your advertising.

53. Charity work

Raising money for charity is a nice thing to do. It's also a great opportunity to market your school and creates a lot of free PR. Send press releases to your local newspaper and radio station and let them know what you are doing to help local charities. Go to Goggle and type "fundraising ideas" if you are not sure where to start.

Your school will not only be doing good things it will also get known locally for its charitable efforts. The respect you earn from the local community will go a long way to attracting the right people to your school.

54. Run FREE seminars for local residents

We run many free seminars for our local community. One of our most popular is a free women's self-defence seminar which we do every few months. It's focused on awareness and reducing risk, with a few kick ass techniques. It helps us break down the common perception that martial arts schools are scary and intimidating to women. Once the seminar has finished many women ask to continue their training in our scheduled classes.

You can run seminars on any topic that will help your local community. Another popular one we offer is a free anti-bullying seminar. Bullying is a big problem right now and we martial artists can offer some unique solutions. Master Dave Kovar has set up a website called "Martial Artists Against Bullying, MAAB". It's a free online resource and it includes information on how to teach an anti-bullying seminar to kids. We regularly get 10-15 children on this course every time we run it.

Go to this website: https://www.donewithbullying.com/

Download all the information, practice it and then set up your own bully prevention seminar. We made a few changes to the course to suit the UK culture, but the information he shares is very good. I think it's a lot better than the advice that most children get from schools at the moment. Plus it makes you feel really good knowing that you are empowering children to stand up to bullying.

55. Word of Mouth

The oldest trick in the book. Talk about what you do to everyone. I've often been sat in a cafe and overheard a conversation between a couple chatting about how they really must start exercising. The right thing to do is to politely interrupt them and introduce yourself and your business, give them a card and invite them to come and try a free class.

Now, that's not always how it works out, often I will overhear the conversation, finish my coffee and go on about my day. Maybe with the attitude that, "I'm not at work now", but that's a missed opportunity as they could turn into long-term students. There are many things that you might overhear that could spark a conversation about what you do.

Talk to as many people as possible. Talk about your business, talk about your students and talk about how martial arts changes lives. People are naturally fascinated by martial arts, so let them know about what you do. Don't forget to give them your business card that you should have in your wallet for such an occasion.

56. Flyers

Flyers do work, but they need to be targeted. It's no good walking house to house posting flyers because you don't know which house will be interested. Instead, I like to think carefully about where my target audience hang out, where they visit and where they live so I can be a bit more targeted with my flyers.

If I'm targeting women, for example, I often put flyers in hairdressers, nail salons, tanning shops and places where women go. For men, its barbers, and sports shops. Think about where your target audience would shop or visit on a regular basis and leave your flyers there. Here's one of our flyers:

If you decide to do door to door flyering make sure you select the right areas based on income and proximity to your school. No point in putting flyers through doors of people who live too far away or who can't afford your classes. Generally, you can expect a 1-2% response from door to door flyering; which is why many instructors are leaving it in preference for more targeted advertising (Facebook etc.).

57. Pre-emptive flying

We all know that gyms & martial arts schools across the country will be sending out their flyers and offers in January hoping to catch all of those New Year resolutions. Why not start your flyer marketing in November offering your January deal?

Get your information out there early and reinforce the message through your social media channels. Frequently the first deal a person receives is the one they act on, so get your seasonal offers out early to beat the competition. Make sure you include an irresistible offer.

58. Anniversaries

Celebrate your school's special anniversaries (1st, 5th, 10th birthdays are good). Organise a black tie dinner, or go to the local pub if you prefer a more informal event. Bringing your members together at a social event is good fun and improves retention as new friendships are built. And of course, you can share your special anniversaries on Facebook and with the local newspaper via a press release.

59. Celebrity endorsement

Unfortunately, we live in the age of the celebrity. We might as well use this fact to our advantage. Do you know any local celebrities, actors, musicians, authors or chefs? Ask them to do a video endorsement for your school in exchange for some free training for their family.

Rightly or wrongly, having someone famous associated with your school will help you get more students. There are several UK based martial arts styles that have even used their connections with Hollywood to get endorsements from A-list celebs, which can't be bad for business.

If you are opening a new full-time centre invite your town's major. This is a news-worthy event so contact your local paper and see if they will send a photographer to cover the opening ceremony.

60. Sponsor a local team

If you sponsor a local sports team, you can have your school's name and website printed on the back of their uniform. If you love sport contact your local teams about how you can help them with sponsorship. It's fun for you supports the local community and gets your name out.

61. Use the upper left

When you pay for print advertising (newspapers, magazines), ensure that you request the upper left corner for you advert. That is where the reader will look first as they turn the page of a newspaper or magazine. **This positioning tends to work better than the bottom right of a page for example.** When placing the order for your print advert specifically request the top left space on the page. It will make a difference to the number of people who see your advert. Make sure your ad includes an attractive image and an irresistible offer.

62. A letter to the editor

Contact your local news editor and talk about how martial arts changes people's lives, how it boosts kid's confidence, gets adults fit and builds a stronger, safer community. Offer your services to the paper in any way they see fit. This will open many doors and create many unexpected opportunities. You might get interviewed by a reporter or you might be invited to write a column for the local paper on safety (like a friend of mine did). Reach out and see what happens.

63. Submit Press Releases

Get to know the sports editor for your local paper. Take them out to lunch and ask them questions about the type of content their paper likes to publish. Once you've got this background information send them press releases about your school, your gradings, guest instructors, your schools anniversaries, competitions your students have won, and the charitable work you do in the local community.

Make sure you present your press release professionally, with correct spelling, grammar, and punctuation. The sports editor doesn't want to spend time correcting your English. Once you've established a working relationship you can send press releases regularly. This is free advertising to a very large audience.

64. Survey your students

Send out regular surveys to your members. Ask them questions like;

What do you enjoy about the classes?

How can we improve the training?
What could we do to make classes better for you?
What attracted you to our school?

Their answers will give you valuable information about what your students want and how it can shape your business moving forward. **You should also use this information to improve your marketing.** For example, if many of your students request late night classes then you can assume there are prospects out there who would also like late night classes.

I like to use an app called TypeForm that allows me to send beautiful, easy to use questionnaires that students complete on the web. This means you can send them via text message, email or share with them on social media.

Check out Typeform here: https://www.typeform.com/

65. Local radio

If you enjoy meeting people and are talkative, radio is another great marketing tool. **Local radio stations are desperate for content so take advantage of this underutilised advertising medium.** Contact your local radio station and talk to them about what you can offer to their listeners. Once you establish a good reputation they will use you again and again. And of course, you can use the fact you've been interviewed on radio in your marketing.

A good time to contact your local radio station is directly after any local event that is newsworthy. For example, if there has been a spate of muggings locally you can offer your services to educate their listeners with tips to keep them safe.

66. Networking groups

Consider joining local community networking groups who organise business breakfasts. **These events are an opportunity for you to meet other business people in your area and exchange information about your services.** If you like meeting people and enjoy talking about your business this is a great way to meet other business owners, get help, share successes and refer each other business.

Over croissants and coffee, you will be able to meet many professionals that can help your business. You may meet osteopaths, physios, and nutritionists to which you can refer your students when they need some extra help. You will also meet plenty of accountants, book-keepers, and lawyers who can help you build your business. **It's a great way to build professional relationships and collaborate on drumming up business locally.**

67. Collaboration

We touched on this subject in the last tip when we talked about networking. **Collaborating with other local businesses will go a long way to increasing your word of mouth marketing.** If you get a sports massage yourself, you can recommend your members to use the same person, likewise, they will recommend your business to their clients. This works for all services and products that compliment your business. Think about services that would benefit your students and their training.

I have collaborative relationships with local physios, masseurs, osteopaths, nutritionists, accountants, health store owners, dentists, sports shops, cafes and more. Make an effort to speak to other business owners about how you can send each other customers.

68. Supplier referrals

Most towns have a local martial arts shop. Get to know the shop owner and ask to your leave business cards and flyers. **Promote the shop to your students and in return, they will refer new clients to your school.** See if you can negotiate a special discount code that your members can use to get money off.

69. Competition time

At the beginning of each year, we run a competition. The 100th member through the door wins a free year of classes. It doesn't need to be a whole year, you could offer a free month or a free pair of gloves, but we've found a year works best for our school. It gets your regular students racing back to class after Christmas and encourages new student enrollments.

This is a great story to share on social media and with your local paper. It draws lots of attention to your school and gets people excited about the possibility of winning a year's free training.

70. Loyalty program

Run a loyalty program that encourages current members to refer new people to your school. For each friend they refer (who joins), you will give them 1% off their training fees for life. If they refer one person they will receive 1% off, if they refer 10 people they will receive 10% off their training fees and so forth.

It works well for both your business and your members. You are offering them a lifetime discount and they are bringing new clients into your school. Even if the original student quits you will still have the friends they referred and the cycle starts again. Test it out and see how it works for you.

71. Branded Balloons

Whenever you are doing demos or community events make sure you have plenty of branded balloons to give away. **If you are trying to speak to parents and the kids are playing up that would be a great time to give them a free balloon.** All kids love a free balloon and it will buy you more time to speak to the parents about your school. After your chat, they will also walk around with your balloon bobbing around for all to see.

72. Tip Sheets

Write a "top ten" tip sheet and share it on social media. Let's say you write "10 Tips On Dealing With Bullies". You could share it on various local Facebook groups (I would start with local parents or mums groups). Try to take advantage of trending topics in your local area.
If, for example, there has been a spate of burglaries in your local area you might want to do "10 Tips On Home Security". **Make sure you include your school's contact information on all tip sheets.** Share them all over social media. Infographics are another interesting way of sharing useful information.

73. Re- Activation Letter

I've probably had over 3000 people come through my school's doors in the last ten years. Of course, not all of them have stayed, or I'd be relaxing on my yacht in the Caribbean right now.

People, for one reason or another quit. Many of these people probably had some unfortunate life event that stopped them training. Maybe they got ill, lost their job or got injured. They fell out of their training routine and didn't come back. **Have you tried inviting them back to training?**

We found a high percentage of people who stopped training would have liked to continue, but they just got out of the habit. All you need to do is contact them and warmly invite them back. Once a year I send all my ex-students a reactivation email or text (we used to send hand written letters but that got too expensive). The content of the re-activation offer is something along the lines of:

"We're sorry that you left our academy. We miss you. We hope that your leaving wasn't anything to do with our teaching or instructors. We'd like to make it up to you in any way possible. Would you be interested in coming back and having a month's free training?

Every year I do this and four or five of our old members come back to start training again. You just need to reach out to them. **Creating a re-activation offer is a great way to bring people back into your school, without having to spend too much energy or money.** Just email your entire list of ex-students with an attractive, time sensitive offer and see who gets back to you.

Or you could dedicate a whole month to re-activating your old students. See pic below:

74. Hang out where your prospects are

Hang out where your target market hangs out. If you know that you attract vegans, go to a vegan cafe. Speak to the owners, get know them and ask to leave your flyers there. If you want more women in your classes, go where women are and speak to them about how martial arts can improve their life. Hang out with your target audience, talk to them about what you do and hand out your business card at every opportunity.

75. Free drinks

If your school is in a high street location, and you have the facilities, you can invite passersby in for a free drink to check out your school. **This works best on very hot or very colds days.** On hot days you can offer iced virgin cocktails (fruit cocktails without alcohol) and on cold days hot chocolate gets people through the doors.

This only works if you have a prime location with lots of passing foot traffic. **Put your most attractive staff on the door and instruct them to invite likely looking people in for a free drink and a tour.**

76. Bulletin / Community board

Most supermarkets and cafes have community bulletin boards where you can post your flyer or business card. Make sure you take your own pins, as there are never any spare ones. If it's somewhere you visit often, check the board frequently. If your advert has gone, replace it with a new one.

77. Local markets

Most towns have farmers/ food/ craft markets that are well attended by the local community. **Use these types of events to distribute your flyers.** Whoever is giving out the flyers needs to be approachable, attractive and able to talk about your school passionately. **You can even rent a pitch at a market and go all out with banners, flags, balloons and students in uniform.** Make sure you bring something interesting to attract people's attention (a free standing punch bag is usually good).

78. Car Stickers

Car stickers are a great way to spread the word about your school, via your members' cars. Use an eye-catching image with a punchy tagline and students will love them. Give them to your students for FREE and let them do your advertising for you.

79. My Life Is My Dojo by Tom Callos

'My life is my dojo' is an idea developed by Martial Arts Master Tom Callos. He shares a lot of fantastic business content via his YouTube channel. Here's the link to his YouTube Channel for martial arts business. It's worth subscribing to:

https://www.youtube.com/watch?v=hyGXKmE4fVw

Let me ask you a question, are your walking your talk? You are a martial arts instructor, so are you in good shape? I was recently teaching a seminar at another school and I was shocked. Every single person in that school was clinically obese. All the black belts, chief instructors, and students were grossly overweight.

I'm used to training with combat athletes: boxers, kickboxers and MMA practitioners, so I'm generally surrounded by people in good shape. But, not all martial artists are like that and there are a lot of "out of shape" martial arts instructors out there.

This doesn't mean that you need to be ripped to run your school. But being grossly overweight certainly affects your ability to talk convincingly about health, exercise, and nutrition. Prospects and students do judge how we instructors look and behave. **To do the best marketing for your school you need to embody the martial arts lifestyle, which means you should keep yourself healthy, fit and trim.** You are a walking example of the martial arts lifestyle.

80. Prepare a good pitch

This is an important one. Have you got a good pitch? **A pitch is your one liner when you are asked a question like, "What do you do?"** Most instructors when asked what they do say something like 'I teach martial arts'. This is OK, but it can be made far more memorable.

If I think the person I'm speaking to shares my sense of humour I usually say:

'I get paid to kick people in the head'. That usually gets a reaction!

If it's more of a formal setting I use a technique I picked up from business coach David Holland. He uses the following method:

Formal person: "So what do you do?"

You: "You know we have a problem in the UK right now with (choose one: obesity, bullying, violence)? Well, I help fix that!"

Formal person: Oh how interesting, how do you do that?

You: Well I... (go onto explain how martial arts helps fix the problem)

Pretty cool eh!

Make sure you tweak your pitch to suit your audience. Your local mayor will require a different pitch than a group of children. **Your pitch is your chance to grab their attention.** If you have a good pitch you will be able to sell the benefits of martial arts to a captivated audience. Work on your pitch, practice it and hone it. You don't get a second chance to make a first impression.

81. Celebrate student's birthdays

We send birthday messages to our students. We used to send actual birthday cards but our school got too big and it became too difficult to manage. Now we send our members a birthday text or Facebook message. It makes your student feel valued because you remembered their birthday.

And of course, they usually thank us publically for taking the time to wish them a happy birthday. **If you are really smart you can give them a little birthday present, such as a voucher to purchase equipment in your pro shop.**

82. Working with local businesses

Many businesses in your town have a budget to maintain the health & fitness of their staff. They encourage their staff to keep fit aiming to promote healthier, happier and more productive employees. If you have the right skills it's worth contacting their human resource department to offer training to their staff.

Depending on your location, this could be at your school or on site at their offices. **You need to ensure all of your materials and resources are presented professionally and ready to go before you make the call to arrange a meeting.**

Do your research about the company and its structure. Many larger businesses are willing to pay big money for a well prepared, structured and organised activity. A friend of mine does a lot of corporate work and the money he charges is obscene. If you can present yourself and your materials to a high standard and make the right contacts, corporate work can be very rewarding.

83. Car park tickets

Most car park tickets have advertising space on the back of the ticket. Usually, the ticket will come out of the machine back first so your advert could be the first thing a prospect sees. **If you put an irresistible offer on the ticket prospects are more likely to pay attention and act upon it.** I have found this to be a surprisingly inexpensive way to market our business locally, with a higher than expected success rate.

When you phone up the ticket company for a quote I would always try to negotiate a lower price. **If they can't reduce the price then don't do it.** From experience, I've always been able to negotiate a deal.

84. Working with Hollywood

When a new martial arts film launches at your local cinema, you can contact the manager and ask to do a short demonstration in the lobby before the film starts. **Cinemas like the extra value a demo provide and are usually willing work with professional martial arts instructors.** There is also a press opportunity to cover your demo and a chance to distribute flyers to the audience of the film. Keep an eye out for the next Kung Fu Panda, Ong Bak, Jackie Chan or Power Rangers film.

85. Write a book

Let's say you were going to choose between two martial art schools. At one of the schools the instructor has written a book about martial arts, and at the other, they haven't. Which one would you choose? All things being equal, probably the one with the book right?

There are few things more impressive than saying "Here's my book". It creates instant authority and respect. If you enjoy writing, I would recommend that you write a book. If like me, you type with one finger it can take a while (it took me nine months to write my first book). If you don't like typing you could transcribe your book instead. Record yourself speaking your book and then find someone online to transcribe it for you. You will then have the first draft of your new book to edit. Transcription is a cheap, quick way to "write" a book.

Another option is to use Dragon Naturally Speaking, (speech recognition software). This allows you to talk out your book into a microphone whilst the software records the words and types them onto your computer screen for you. Pretty neat eh. Here's the link:

http://www.nuance.co.uk/dragon/index.htm

Writing a book massively increases your exposure as a professional. There are hundreds of martial arts schools and thousands of martial art instructors in the UK, but very few have actually written a book. **By writing a book you put**

yourself in a very elite group. And you can use this in your marketing.

I am the only instructor in the UK, (that I am aware), who has written several books about martial arts business specifically for the UK market. As you can imagine, this has opened various doors that would have been shut to me. So, if you enjoy writing get started on your book today. Message me if you need any help with this as I have a lot of experience in self-publishing.

86. Open events

Open events are when you invite the local community to come to your school. They can chat to an instructor, book a 10-minute taster session and get a tour of your school. This requires lots of pre-event marketing and you will need to plan everything well in advance. It's no good organising an open evening two weeks before it's due to start. You don't have enough time to excite people about the event. You will need to create a social media campaign, print and deliver flyers, write a press release and more to make sure people turn up.

Giving enough lead time will also make sure you can fit into people's busy schedules. If you advertise four to six weeks in advance it's likely they will still have time free to fit in a visit to your school. Respect people's time and give them plenty of advance warning.

87. Kung Fu Panda Costume

Kids LOVE the Kung Fu Panda. We bought a Kung Fu Panda costume on eBay from China for about £150 (see pic below). Every Saturday during summer I pay one of my students, (I used to do this myself, but now I have the budget to pay someone to wear the costume), to walk around town, with a friend handing out flyers.

It's amazing. Kids will walk through walls to get a picture with our Kung Fu Panda. **I dress him in a club t-shirt, pose with the kids, and let the parents take a pic (which no doubt they share on social media). Make sure you give them a flyer and invite them to a free trial class.** It works and is a fun way to get your name around the town.

The costume has paid for itself several times over. So if you have a few mature teen students who want to earn some extra cash at the weekends, I suggest you get a Kung Fu Panda outfit NOW.

88. Roadside billboards

Billboards are very expensive, but they do work if you have a great offer at the right time. You can expect to pay between £200 - £500 a month for a billboard depending on its size and location. Try to negotiate on the price as you may get a good deal. Make sure the poster is professionally designed with an attractive image and a catchy headline.

On page 88 is an example of one of our billboard ads. **As you can see there isn't much text as people driving past don't have time to read it.** Let the image and headline sell the advert. Billboards are an expensive tool, but worth considering in the right location with the right offer.

89. Trailer signs

Trailer signs are trailers that feature big posters advertising a business. **These are towed to different locations and parked to attract the attention of passing motorists.** Sometimes you are able to rent the trailer yourself and take it to the specific locations you want. Other companies will print your advert, attach it to the trailer and tow it to your desired location. I see quite a lot of these around my town.

This could be a good way to make your school more visible locally, especially if your location is poor. In the UK a lot of full-time schools are located on industrial estates away from houses, so a trailer (with a great image and your info) can help make people aware of your business. Trailers are often cheaper than billboards so they may be a cost-effective way to test this type of visual marketing.

90. Give Away

Free Stuff

Always have something free to give to people that come into your school. Kids, for example, love stickers, they are inexpensive and act as a reminder of your school later. Keyring's, fridge magnets and pens also work well. Include your contact details on any items you give away. It will remind them of your school after they have left. No one should leave your school empty handed.

91. Cash Outs

Generally, I advise school owners to only take payments for classes via standing order or direct debit. **This regulates your income, makes budgeting easier for your students and gives you a measure of security.** However, some prospects are put off by direct debits. You can make an exception for these people and let them pay cash for their training fees. **I only accept cash for six to twelve months in advance.** I don't want to be chasing students for cash after each class, so I only offer cash deals for longer periods.

Each year we offer twenty students the chance to pay for a whole year training for a discount. A certain percentage of your students love a deal and will snap this up and pay immediately. This is useful if you need some quick cash to do renovations or buy some new equipment. Just don't spend the money on a holiday to Bali, (remember you owe these people a years' worth of training). **Re-invest the money back into your business.**

92. Parent and child classes

There are not many activities where parents and children are able to take part together. **Family martial arts classes are one way to do this.** Parents get to spend time with their kids and the children love to watch their parents trying to keep up with them. Family classes are not for everyone and it depends on your members and the space available, but it can work really well. I know several schools that only run family classes. **Just make sure that parents only train with their own kids and that everything is monitored for safety.**

Ask your members if they would like this type of class. Family classes are very useful for parents who don't have access to childcare, so have to find activities they can do with their kids.

93. Family Discount

If you are a school which attracts both children and their parents, a family discount is a great way to bring a whole family in and make it affordable. The discount you offer usually depends on how many family members are looking to join. **At my school, I only offer a discount if three or more family members want to join.** But I know some schools offer a discount on the second family member. It's up to you. You have to test and see what works best for you. Make sure you use family discounts in your advertising.

94. Discounts for emergency services

Offer discounts to your local soldiers, firemen, policemen and ambulance workers. **They do an amazing job and deserve a discount.** They also have jobs that require them to be physical and need to be active to perform at their best. This means they are conscious about their health and fitness.

Another thing to note with this type of client is that they work shifts. This means that they may need to train at odd times. To cater for this you will need to have daytime and late night sessions available. **There are several websites out there that share special discounts for public service staff so put your info out there.** Plus emergency service staff tend to generate a lot of referrals as they are generally close and look after each other. Here's a good site to start:

http://www.forcesdiscount.com/

95. Waive your joining fee

This is something you can promote to entice new members into your school. Many people don't like paying joining fees so waiving the joining fee works well as a marketing tactic. I wouldn't recommend doing this all year as the joining fee should cover your advertising costs. Make it a limited time offer during your quieter months, For example, 'No joining fee in August' works well.

96. Grading Events

Make your gradings a community event, rather than a private test. American school owners know how to do this best. After their gradings, they often hire a hotel ballroom and throw a big celebratory party. They invite the extended family, local community members and dignitaries. They have presentations, awards, and speeches.

I'm not suggesting that you blow your entire profit on throwing the party of the year, but try organizing an event where students can celebrate with their family and friends. Gradings (especially for Black Belt) mean a lot to your students and should be celebrated. **Plus because students can invite their extended family and friends it's a great marketing opportunity as well.**

97. Win Awards

Enter your business into local and national business awards. If you win you get massive bragging rights. If you lose you can mention you were a runner-up in a prestigious competition.

Imagine if you were awarded 'UK Martial Arts School" I am certain it would generate a lot of attention for your business. So go out there and enter your business into local, regional and national competitions. What have you got to lose?

98. Groupon and voucher sites

If you have a particularly quiet class that you can't fill, consider using offer websites, such as Groupon or Wowcher. These sites offer special discounted deals on goods and services. Make your offer exclusive to the class you are looking to fill. You don't want a load of deal hunters in your most profitable classes. Use these "deal sites" to fill your quieter classes and sign them up to your regular classes once the deal expires.

99. Birthday Parties

This is not for the faint-hearted. Kids birthday parties can be a good way to earn some extra money, attract new students and have a lot of fun. But I have to mention that they can be really hard work. Work out your expenses and calculate how many children you need to make it viable. When we ran kids birthday parties we required a minimum of 15 new kids to make it financially worthwhile. You provide a couple of hours of instruction and entertainment and the parents bring the food, cake, and refreshments.

For those children that have never visited your academy before it's an opportunity to give them a fun taste of martial arts. Make sure you have a special time-sensitive offer for the new kids after the party. Give it to the parent who picks them up, or include it in their goodie bag.

If you are really desperate for students you could even offer FREE birthday parties as a marketing strategy. Kids birthday parties can cost upwards of £500 so offering a free space and tuition in order to get 20 new kids into your academy is a win / win situation. The parents get a fun and cheap birthday party and you get to market to 20 kids and their parents and siblings. Worth considering!

BONUS IDEAS!

Here are some bonus ideas to get more students into your school.

100. Multiplying your marketing message

It's important to get your marketing out to your local community consistently, whether its flyers, a branded t-shirt, a free seminar or a Facebook advert. Your marketing needs to be continuous so that you are seen repeatedly by those seeking martial arts classes in your area. **Flyers, for example, usually require multiple exposures to work effectively.**

This is because your prospect might get the first flyer at a point where they are not ready to consider martial arts. But six months later, everything might have changed. Flyers usually require repeat exposure to work effectively (which can be expensive).

Your goal is to keep your school at the top of people's minds when they are thinking about anything martial arts related. That could mean fitness, self-defence, bullying, weight loss or competition. We want our local community to think of us first! Keep marketing using multiple channels (Facebook, google, flyers, press releases, demos) to keep your school front of mind.

101. Communicating your USP

You need to differentiate yourself from your competition or otherwise prospects will choose which school to join based on price. In marketing, your difference is commonly known as your "Unique Selling Proposition" (USP).

Your USP is what makes your school different/ better than all your competitors.

Do you know what your Unique Selling Position is?

If not, answer these questions

- What is unique about you and your school?
- What do you do differently from your competitors?
- Do you offer specific services that others don't?

- Why should someone choose you over your competitors?
- What makes you unique in your town?

Answer these questions and they will help you form your USP, which you can use in your marketing. For example, one of our USP's is our relaxed and friendly atmosphere. We don't use titles, everyone calls each other by their first name, bowing is kept to a minimum and we tell jokes and have fun in our classes. This attracts a certain type of person to our school and sets our schools tone. **What's your USP and how can you use it in your marketing?**

Summary & Action Plan

There you go, 101 ways to get a student. Like I said in the introduction you need to focus on the 80/20 principle when it comes to selecting which marketing techniques to use. Here are some things to consider:

- What's the 20% of this list that will give you 80% of your enquiries?
- What are the most cost effective ideas? (FREE is best to start with)
- What do you enjoy doing? (As you will be more likely to do it every week)

It's your job to go through each of these marketing methods and test to see which ones work best for you and your business.

I would start with all the ideas that don't cost any money first before you move onto those that require spending your hard earned cash. For most schools that means referrals, building a good sales website and getting that website on the first page of Google. After that what you choose is up to you.

I'm reluctant to share my favourite strategies because they may not work for you. You need to discover for yourself what works best for you.

Next Steps

What I would like you to do now is go back through the book and circle the top ten ideas that you can implement cheaply and easily. Make a list of them. These will be your weekly marketing basics. **These are the things you will do week in week out, for as long as you run a martial arts school.** Test which ones work best and swap any that under-perform.

Once you have a list of 10 core marketing activities that you know work, schedule them in your diary or planner. For example, Monday could be "referral day" where you focus on generating referrals. Tuesday could be your social media day when you schedule your weekly posts. Wednesday could be flyer day where you distribute flyers to your target market. By scheduling your marketing it becomes a habitual part of your daily routine like brushing your teeth.

Once you have your weekly marketing planned, next you need to look at seasonal marketing activities. This is where you plan all the events throughout the year you are looking to run: Easter events, Halloween events, Summer demos, Short courses throughout the year, Grading ceremonies, Open days, New Year deals etc. Put them all in the diary and schedule two to four weeks for prep and advertising. **I like to use a wall planner for this so I can see my whole years marketing mapped out.**

You should now have daily, weekly and monthly marketing activities planned ahead for the year. Follow the plan and make sure you are testing each advertising tactic to see how cost effective they are.

Anything that consistently underperforms should be dropped and replaced by a new marketing tactic. If you keep testing you will eventually come up with a solid marketing plan that works like clockwork.

The secret to making these tips work is getting into a habit. **You should market EVERY SINGLE DAY.**

Funnily enough, the more consistent your marketing, the better results you get.

Remember students will always leave for one reason or another, it's the nature of our business. If you want to grow, you need to ensure that you are doing enough effective marketing not just to maintain your numbers, but to grow your business steadily. This takes planning AND execution.

Marketing your school is not rocket science.

It's simply doing the right things, at the right time, even if you don't feel like it.

Good luck!

Don't forget to test all the ideas and take ACTION EVERY DAY!

Matt Chapman
Black Belt Biz

10 WEEKLY COST EFFECTIVE MARKETING ACTIVITIES

List the 10 weekly marketing activities you are going to do EVERY week

1.

2.

3.

4.

5.

6.

7.

8.

9.

10.

Notes:

WEEKLY MARKETING PLANNER

Now take your 10 marketing activities and split them over the week. Write down what you are going to do each day.

Keep this on your phone and print it out (stick it where you will see it every day). This is the minimum marketing you will do each week. **Note I said the minimum.**

The more marketing you do the better your results!

MONDAY:

TUESDAY:

WEDNESDAY:

THURSDAY:

FRIDAY:

SAT & SUN:

30 RETENTION STRATEGIES

FOR MARTIAL ARTS SCHOOLS

Retention is key when you want to grow your martial arts business. There is no point recruiting 100 new clients only to lose 101 the following month. That is hard work and stressful. Attracting new students will also eat up all of your time and keep you away from what you really want to be doing, teaching martial arts.

Your chief goal is to get and keep students for as long as possible. Not only is it good for your business as a martial artist, but it's also good for your student as the longer they stay the fitter and more skilled they get.

In this book, we are going to look at many retention strategies that will help you keep your students for longer, which will, in turn, stabilise the growth of your martial arts business.

QUICK REFERENCE

Leaky Buckets
Attrition
Seasonal Variations in Attrition
Lifetime Student Value
Unmotivated Instructors
7 Reasons why people quit martial arts
Tracking Attendance
ABC Students
Missing In Action Calls / Texts
Retention zones
Your ideal student
Pre-framing prospects to become lifelong students
Encouraging prospects to turn up to their trial class
The importance of a PAR - Q and information form
Using NLP to create rapport with new students
The six human needs and martial arts
Mentoring
Spend time with your students
Set a grading date as soon as possible
3 points of contact
Get them to invest in equipment
2, 4 & 6 weeks follow up calls
The TLC program
Send helpful emails to support their first 100 days
Praise
Ask for Student feedback
Create separate Facebook groups
Sharing other peoples content to help your students
Demo teams / Fight teams
Share Motivational Material
Create a top heavy syllabus
Use a character education program
Gradings boost retention
Family discounts
Catch-up gradings
Boost retention by creating an online martial arts school
Offer Home Training Routines
The Martial Arts Instructors Dilemma
Host extra curricular seminars
Run outdoor training
Re-activating ex-students
Celebrating Firsts
Conclusion
Find out more

LEAKY BUCKETS

I like to think of martial arts schools as leaky buckets. You invest time and money advertising to new students (pouring them into your bucket). Over time these students leak out of the holes in your bucket. So you work harder to recruit more students and pour them back into the top of your bucket, only for them to drip out of the holes once again. This cycle continue's year after year. The more holes you have in your bucket, the more ways your students will leak out of them.

The holes in your bucket are any reason why your students quit.

They include :

- Injuries
- Illness
- Move away
- Work commitments
- Family issues
- Financial issues
- Boredom
- Lack of short & long term goals
- Indifference from instructor

If we can work to seal some of these holes in your bucket, your student numbers will go up. This is retention.

The leaky bucket analogy is a nice simple way to think about how your martial arts school works. Your school is the bucket, new students get poured in the top and the holes are the various reasons, problems and excuses that cause them to quit.

My aim, with the information in this book, is to help you plug up some, if not all of those holes. To help you find solutions as to why students stop training, therefore keeping your retention levels high.

Retention is the ability to keep your students training for as long as possible. That's what we all want, right? We want to keep our student's training with us for as long as possible. Hopefully, you already have students who have been training with you for 5 - 10 years. Those are the students we want, and as many of them as possible. It makes our life easier. It makes teaching more enjoyable sharing with people that are loyal and have stuck around.

However, at the end of the day, everyone quits at one point or another. Yes, even us martial art die hards who choose martial arts as a career. It's just we will quit when we drop dead on the mat. Many students will quit after their first session. They come, they try it, they don't like it and they quit. Chances are they won't tell you that it's not for them, they just won't turn up again. They are done with martial arts and decide that Zumba is more their thing. That's ok though, martial arts is not for everyone, and you wouldn't want a class full of half-hearted students. Not everyone likes to come to a place where like minded people enjoy punching and kicking each other. It takes a special type of nutter.

Some students will stay for 1 month, others 3 months, a year, 2 years, 5 years, 15 years and so on. What we aim to do is maximise the time your students stay with you. Sometimes as instructors we are guilty of letting students quit without questions or feedback.

To run our schools profitably it's important to have systems in place, some of them automated, that will solve many of the problems that cause your students to quit. It's important to see the many holes in your bucket and plug them with tested systems and solutions. This will increase your student retention and keep your students training at your school for longer.

ATTRITION

Attrition is the rate at which you lose students each week, month or year. The average attrition rate in martial arts schools in the UK is between 4% and 8%.

If your school attrition rate is below 4%, that is amazing! Your school is really rocking. Keep doing what you are doing as its working. I know some schools that have a 2% attrition rate (which is really low). It's possible to get those percentages down, but you are never going to get them to zero. Certainly not on a regular basis. I've never had a month go past that someone hasn't left and I've been teaching martial arts for 20 years. Things happen which are beyond your control that will cause your students to quit. They get ill, injured or they move out of the area. That's just life.

If your attrition rate goes above 8%, you are in big trouble, because you are losing students too fast and it's going cause a major problem for your business moving forward. It's very hard to grow your school if you are losing more than 8% of your students each month. This is because if you want to grow you will have to replace the 8% and then add more in order to expand.

How do I work out my attrition percentage?

I know you might be thinking

"Er, but I don't know my attrition percentage"

Fortunately, there is a simple calculation you can use to work it out.

1. First you need to know the number of students that quit over a month.
2. Then divide that number by your total number of students
3. And then times that number by 100.

For example, here's this months calculation for my school:

1. Number of students that quit= 16
2. Divided by 350 (total number of students)
3. x 100 = 4.6% attrition rate (meaning 4.6 % of my school quit that month)

Now work out your attrition rate here: ___________________________________

One of the most important things you can do for your business is working out your attrition rate. Once you have this information you can decide what you need to do and formulate a plan of action. If, for example, you have 100 students and your attrition rate is around 4% you know that you need to keep an eye on things. You will lose 4 students a month, but if you are signing up 6 a month your school will grow (slowly).

If your attrition rate comes closer to the 8% then you know that you need to change what you are doing. You are losing 8 students a month and that makes it much harder to grow. You need to find the leaky holes in your bucket and take immediate action.

Knowing your attrition each month will help you manage and grow your business. This, in turn, translates to less stress and more enjoyment teaching martial arts. Knowing these numbers will also help you understand how many students you need to attract and keep in order to grow your business.

If you have 100 students and are losing between 4 to 8 students a month, you know, in order to grow you will need to sign up between 6 to 10 students. My school has roughly 360 students. We typically lose 12 to 18 students per month. So just to stay even, we need to sign up that same number of students each month. We actually aim to sign up 20 to 25 a month, so that we are growing our student base and not just maintaining.

Seasonal Variations in Attrition

There are common times of the year where attrition increases for most martial arts schools. Summer, for example, is generally a time where many schools lose students, mostly due to holidays and people wanting to spend more time outside in the warmer weather. Leading up to Christmas through to January, many people feel the strain on their wallets. Others have booked their diary solid with parties that take them away from your school.

There are many solutions which can help keep those people in your school. For example, if someone is struggling financially to attend your school you could offer them a discount for a specific period. Because if they quit, (if only for a month or two), they often quit for life. Sometimes it is better to keep them in training, albeit at a reduced rate, than cancelling their payment and never seeing them again.

In this case, it's much easier and more cost effective to work out a "deal" to keep that student training, than it is to find, recruit and sign up a new student. You will need to have a conversation with the student and explain the situation and that you are able to help them keep training. Not only will it encourage them to keep training, but you will be sending out a positive message about how much you care for them as a member of your school. However, if you do offer a discount make sure the student is aware that this only for a limited time (typically a month or two).

At my school, we also run a lot of internal promotions during the times when numbers typically drop. This includes outdoor training sessions, special social events, free seminars and workshops and attendance competitions. All these tactics encourage your students to keep turning up during the quieter times of the year.

Jot down a few activities you could schedule to keep students training here:

1.

2.

3.

4.

5.

LIFETIME STUDENT VALUE

Every martial arts school owner needs to know what their lifetime student value is. It's important to remember that when you sign up a new student, there is a possibility that they will be training with you for 10+ years. Each new student that comes through your doors has the potential to be the student who sticks around for a decade or longer. That is, they will provide 10+ years of revenue for you and your school. Using this time frame as an example work out how much value that holds when you add up their training fees, seminars, gradings, private lessons and equipment purchases over 10 years. It will give you a ball park figure of the lifetime value of that particular student. This a great illustration of how important each student is and the value they have to your business.

Let me show you why this important.

I visited a martial arts school in Portsmouth a few years back. When I walked in, the coaches were grappling on the mats. They looked at me and then continued with their training. Being a martial artist, I'm pretty familiar with weird personalities, so I decided to wait. I waited and waited, 10 minutes later they hadn't even said as much as a hello or welcomed me into their school, so I left.

Can you see how in this instance, there is a possibility that they just lost 15 years of potential revenue for their business, just because they didn't greet me when I arrived. A simple 'hello' or 'we are just finishing up, be with you in a couple of minutes' would have been much more positive, than no communication at all.

Unfortunately, this type of situation happens in a lot of martial art schools. I recently had a similar problem in my school. A lady came in to enquire about starting our classes, she appeared to be quite nervous and had a lot of questions. I booked her in for her first session at a later date. When she arrived for her trial class, I was tied up teaching a class. I acknowledged her arrival with a nod and signalled that I'd be over in a minute. I wasn't able to abandon the students I was teaching and hoped that would be enough to reassure her to take a seat till I was free from the class. She still looked extremely nervous. I turned my attention back to my students for a short moment and when I looked back she had gone.

I tried to call and text her but got no response. It was obvious that she was uncomfortable in my school and thought, "this is not for me" and left. So in that situation, maybe I too lost a lifetime student.

We will cover the importance of meeting, greeting and creating a welcoming first impression later in the book.

I would like you to think about your Lifetime Student Value. Can you work out the value of one of your typical students? How long does the average student stay and how much do they invest in their training over that time? Work it out now, it may well change the way you view each new enquiry.

If your typical student stays for 6 months, add up all of the money they will pay you for that length of time to find out their LSV. This will give you a figure to work from. Imagine if you were able to extend that typical student into being one that trains with you for a year, or 5 years. How much more extra revenue that would bring to your business?

UNMOTIVATED INSTRUCTORS

Many instructors lack motivation when they have to teach a class of new students. They don't feel like its worth their time to teach beginners when they will probably quit anyway. I believe the opposite is true, the majority of these beginners quit because they are not being treated the way they deserve. They will see more advanced students receiving more attention and feel like they are being ignored. Treat your students well from day one and they are far more likely to stand by you for the next 15 years.

There is a nice rhyme I teach my assistant teachers, who often at the beginning of their journey don't like to teach beginners;

"They're not an annoying pest, they're a welcome guest".

You need to be happy to see new students when they come through the door and encourage them throughout their class. Your enthusiasm will rub off on to them, especially if they are nervous or unsure. Your positivity will help put them at ease and provide reassurance that they made the right decision in coming to your school. If in their first session you don't treat them well, it's almost guaranteed they won't be back for another class. Plus they're unlikely to refer you to their friends, and definitely won't talk about you positively on social media. This may sound like common sense advice, but it's surprising how many of us slip up on these basic ground rules of how to treat someone coming to your school for the first time.

7 REASONS WHY PEOPLE QUIT MARTIAL ARTS

This is not an exclusive list, you may have some other reasons that you would like to add, but these are the most common reasons why people quit. These are also the ones that I think we can address which will help the retention of your students and grow your business.

1. INJURIES :

Injuries are very common at the beginning of a students training journey. During the first few months of starting a new activity, especially if they have been inactive before, it's easy to tweak a joint, injure a ligament or hurt themselves in many comical ways.

What can we do about injuries? Firstly we need to ensure that the level of the class they are taking is appropriate for their fitness and abilities. For example, I don't let beginners do certain exercises and I don't allow sparring during their first six months. They are not ready for contact yet, and they will either get injured physically or emotionally.

We train with prevention in mind, so we look for signs of over training and avoid ballistic or plyometric movements. We also look for trends in injuries. We went through a period where a lot of women in our classes were getting calf injuries. It took a little investigation as to what was going on. In the end, we figured out that many women wear heels all day long and then come training. As soon as they took their heels off they would over stretch their shortened calf muscles and pull a muscle. We introduced calf stretches at the beginning and end of our classes to help combat this problem and it hasn't raised its ugly head since.

We also don't do any explosive exercises in the first months. These exercises are often too hard on a beginners body and can lead to all sorts of muscles and tendon injuries which would stop them from training. If a student gets injured during the first three months of their training they are very unlikely to come back. Injury prevention is the key here. Spend time talking to beginners about the importance of warming up, cooling down and stretching to help prevent injuries. Educate your students on safe training techniques.

2. WORK COMMITMENTS :

Your student changes their job, they lose their job or their hours of work change. Any of these things can affect how often your students attend classes, or if they take the decision to quit as they put their work first.

What can we do with conflicting work commitments? You can keep your schedule of classes flexible, to give those with unusual hours a chance to train at different times. It's also an opportunity to offer private lessons or home routines as these options are more time flexible. If they lose their job or their hours are cut, you can offer them a temporary deal where their membership fees are also reduced or cut. It's important that you help students in their time of need, as this creates a lot of goodwill. I would like to highlight that this should only be for a fixed time, no one should train for free indefinitely. You could also put them to work, cleaning the mat, helping out in classes or handing out promotional material in exchange for training for an agreed period.

3. FAMILY COMMITMENTS :

Kids, school trips, and sickness all affect whether students can come to training. Many children also have clubs after school so are less likely to commit to other activities such as martial arts.

What can we do with family commitments? Firstly, you can encourage the whole family to be involved in training at your school (assuming that you have classes for both children and adults). A flexible timetable will help family members to be able to schedule classes around their busy lives. Create family discount packages to encourage the whole family to get involved. If you don't already, offer family classes where the whole family trains together, (kids and adults at the same time). This reduces childcare costs and gives the family a fun fitness activity they can share.

4. FINANCIAL ISSUES :

Your student or their partner may have lost their job and its putting financial strain on their expenses. Maybe they have moved house and the new mortgage is taking its toll. There are many reasons why a financial issue could upset their training routine.

What can we do to help ease financial issues? Firstly you'll need to know what the issue is. Not the ins and outs of someone's financial situation, but if they come to you and tell you that they will need to stop training as they are currently out of work, then you can help by giving them subsidised or free training for a fixed period. This creates loyalty as the student realises you are not in it just for the money and genuinely care.

5. CHANGE OF LOCATION :

This could be that the person has moved house, or that you have moved the location of your school. Maybe the parking is not as good, or it's further to drive.

What can we do if your student or your school changes location? If your student is moving to another county then it's clear that they won't be training with you on a regular basis anymore, but you can help them by recommending a new school for them in their new area. This reinforces their trust in you and your school and they will continue to recommend you to their friends and family.

If the location of your school changes you need to be as excited as possible about the new location and communicate clearly how it will benefit the students. Consider what steps to take to make the transition easier for your students. Try to make things as convenient as possible. People can be lazy and if things are not easy they might stop coming. Talk to your students about the change of location and how you can help.

6. ACHIEVED THEIR GOALS :

At the beginning of your student's training, they may have had a goal to reach a certain belt level, or to lose a certain amount of weight. Often, once a goal is met they are not able to look beyond that goal or objective and their motivation drops, so they quit.

What can we do if they have achieved their goals? It's time for a review and to set new goals. It's a chance to have a discussion to point out other things they might like to achieve. You have been in martial arts a long time, so you know how much there is to learn. The black belt, for example, is not the end goal, its the start of students learning. Pre-frame your senior grades about this so they are prepared.

Or perhaps they might be interested in becoming an instructor? In which case it's a great time to introduce them to your Instructor Training Programme.

Maybe they want to get into competition? We have a structured process for students to try out for our school's fight team. This provides a challenging goal to work towards.
Talk to your students regularly to set new goals.

7. BOREDOM :

Nowadays people are easily bored. If you do a lot of the same drills, movements and sequences time after time, your students will tire and start looking for other distractions or for the next fad.

What can we do about boredom? We know that in martial arts repetition is essential to master any skill. But do we have to teach the same drills day after day? No, it's possible with creativity and planning to teach the same set of movements but in different ways.

Disguising repetition is a fabulous skill to develop and it will keep your students coming back for more. It also makes teaching classes more challenging for you as you have to come up with new ideas and variations to keep your students motivated.

My pad drill website mittmaster.com is all about teaching fun and exciting classes by disguising repetition. Check it out here: www.mittmaster.com

8. INSTRUCTORS WITH BIG EGOS :

When martial arts was first introduced to this country you were not allowed to speak to your chief instructor. You needed to ask a junior level instructor to pass on your questions. Thankfully these days things are different and the relationship between instructors and students is better and both parties converse openly.

What can we do about instructors egos? Make yourself open and approachable. You need to be able to talk to your students and your students talk to you. Be interested in their development and praise where praise is due. During training use their name to let them know they are doing something well. If you have a large school, it's hard to remember everyone's names, but it goes a long way to making people feel included and part of the team.

Keep tabs on your assistant instructors. Ensure that they are following your teaching methods with how they present themselves and communicate with the students. Try to resolve any issues as soon as they arise. Letting small problems fester will lead to much bigger problems later down the line. Make sure your assistants understand whose school it is, so they follow your rules.

9. JEALOUSY AND COMPETITION :

I'm sure you are familiar with this situation - You have a young student who double grades at one grading. Another parent notices this and reacts badly as they feel their child is not getting the same treatment.

What can you do about jealousy? I think that you have two choices. You can answer their concerns or not. Personally, I favour answering their question in an open and friendly manner. There may be many factors as to why one child double grades. Maybe the child in question attends more sessions than the other, or maybe they have previous experience that the other doesn't. Whatever the reason you can explain it to the disgruntled parent. It's not a bad reflection on their child it's just that each child is different and they are being assessed separately. Ultimately your decision is final, whether they accept your explanation or not. Just try to communicate calmly and professionally.

10. LOSS OF MOTIVATION :

This is a classic and happens a lot. As instructors, we know that motivation is something that comes and goes, but your students may not be aware of this. Kids especially easily lose motivation. Their minds change often and they are influenced by what their friends are doing. Keeping them hooked on any activity is a challenge, but extremely rewarding when you get it right.

What can we do about a loss of motivation? It's important to communicate from the very beginning (pre-framing) that as your students progress through their training there will be times where their motivation will decline. This is a temporary phase and is part of dedicating their time to learning any new skill. You can reassure them that when they do have these dips in motivation you will be there to help them and keep them on track. You could offer them a free 15-30 minute private session to work on things which they are finding difficult or schedule a 15-minute goal setting assessment. Setting new short term goals is a simple way to get your students on track (and is easy to monitor, so they can see their progress).

You can usually see when someone's motivation is waning as they start to complain more and their attendance becomes spotty, so pay attention and speak to those that need help.

TRACKING ATTENDANCE

Speaking of attendance it's really important to track who turns up to class each week. If you are not tracking who is coming to your classes it's impossible to know how many people are starting or leaving at any given time. As the size of your school increases the importance of tracking attendance increases. Without this important information you won't be able to calculate your attrition rates and you won't know how many people you will need to recruit to grow your school. Tracking attendance is easy when you have 10 students but very difficult once you pass 50 active members.

Your attendance data is also really useful when someone disappears for a couple of sessions or weeks. You will be able to notice these absences early on and should be able to address any issues that might be brewing.

There are 3 easy ways to track attendance:

1. Software (Online or offline): creating a database for your school.
2. Attendance cards: where students can log themselves into a class when they arrive.
3. Register: where you will do a roll call at the beginning of class, ticking off names.

There was a time early on that we didn't track our students, attendance or their payments. We found out much later that one of our students hadn't been making any payments for well over a year. We spoke to him and explained that he owed us £1200, or thereabouts. He did pay us eventually, as we arranged manageable instalments for him. This was a big wake-up call and since then we have tracked attendance.

You will need to do some testing and see which system (online, cards or register) works best for you and is within your price range. Regardless of which system you use you must track your student's attendance daily. Without doing this you won't have any chance to manage your attrition.

ABC STUDENTS

Once you have a database of students you will need to "grade" them. I'm not talking about awarding belts here, I'm talking about an ABC grade that will help you easily monitor those students that need a little help.

A STUDENTS :

A, Students are the ones that don't need any motivating or encouragement. They are practically living in your school. They turn up to every class, arrive early and stay after class to chat with their classmates. You wouldn't be able to get rid of them if you tried. These are your A students, these are the students you want to try to have most of.

B STUDENTS :

B students are committed students, they are consistent and they like to train hard. They may take time out if they get injured or go away on holiday, but they are likely to keep you informed when that happens. These are also great students to have. It would take a little work to turn them into A students which would be ideal, as once converted they would require even less work.

C STUDENTS :

These students are the ones that are thinking about quitting. They are on the edge. Their attendance is sporadic, and are not motivated when they arrive in class. They don't engage well with other members of your school and it's clear to see that they are not feeling good about their decision to be there. Your C students are your main priority. You need to spend extra time with these students, you need to call them when they miss classes, you need to help them set goals and stay on track. You need to look at ways that you can convert them into B students and then ultimately into A students.

You can label your students A, B or C on your register or database so that you are able to monitor them on a regular basis, within your classes. I write A, B, C next to their name in our register. This helps make us aware of where they are and allows us to focus on the C's when teaching.

Take some time now to write down some of your student's names that come to mind that fit within the A, B or C grades. Then when you have a moment, do this exercise for all of your members. Once this is completed, make a list of B and C students and start the process of upgrading them to become B and A students.

MISSING IN ACTION CALLS/ TEXTS

We use attendance cards in our school and we like to monitor our student's attendance on a weekly basis. This means that we check our attendance cards once a week and those students who haven't ticked any of the classes on their cards have not attended that week. This means that we can send them a short text asking if they are ok. Typically 90% of them get back to us with a reason why they haven't been in. If there is a problem we can arrange a time to speak to them to see if we can help to find a solution. It's a way of nipping problems in the bud early and addressing any issues that student might have.

Schedule a weekly MIA session to chase up those students who haven't trained that week.

RETENTION ZONES

There are 3 retention zones that you need to be aware of. Each zone comes with its own problems and issues.

1. DANGER ZONE :

The danger zone covers the first 12 months of training. It's called the danger zone as its the time when students are most likely to quit. Maybe martial arts is not what they thought it would be and they have decided it's not for them. Maybe sparring got a little heavy one session and it puts them off their training. Or they injured themselves and never came back. Most people quit martial arts during the first six months.

2. BOREDOM ZONE :

This zone sits between 12 months and 3 years. The students in this zone have been training with you for a while are likely to get bored. They might be thinking, "I've been training the same stuff now for over a year, I really want to be doing this and that". You need to keep an eye on these boredom zone students as you don't want them slipping. They'll need a bit of guidance to keep them on track. Add variety to your classes and set new goals to help move them up to the next zone.

3. LIFESTYLE ZONE :

This zone is for your students who have been training for 3 years plus. These guys are in it for the long haul and you need to ensure that they stay in that frame of mind. The are committed and are working towards their black belts or have expressed an interest in becoming instructors at some point. Students who pass three years training tend to stick around for a long time.

Looking at these three zones, its clear that the majority of your time should be spent on those in the danger zone. Because there is no point in focusing on long-term retention if students don't make it through the first couple of months. As they start to progress and the longer you keep them training, they will start to move up to the next zone. You need to get them to the point where they understand that martial arts has such a positive impact on the way they live, that they can't do without it.

Keeps these zones in mind when you think about your students.

Which zone are they currently in and what can you do to help them?

___

___

___

___

___

___

___

___

___

___

___

YOUR IDEAL STUDENT

Have you ever thought about who is your ideal student? Try to think about gender, age and location. How much do they earn? Do they have children? What job do they have? What TV do they like to watch? What do they like to do in their spare time? What goals do they have?

This may seem like a silly exercise, but its a really important one. Knowing who your ideal student is will give you all the information you need to make your marketing more specific. If you are advertising to everyone in your local area don't be surprised by the strange mix of prospects you attract. If you can specifically market to your ideal student, you will be happier with the type of person you are attracting to your school. You will get them and they will get you and they are much more likely to stick around longer.

For example, I don't really like teaching children. So, although we have a children's program, I don't teach the kids classes and I target my advertising towards adults. I like teaching adults, so I want to attract more adults to my school.

I also prefer to work with women who have plenty of free time. They can afford the training, they invest in seminars and equipment and they have spare time to train. I also like working with women as they are smarter than men (sorry guys). They don't have egos and won't try to knock my head off when we are sparring.

Once you know who your ideal student is all your marketing should be aimed specifically towards them. Don't make your adverts general. Get really specific. I target my ads to women in my local area, aged 20-50 who are into fitness and health. If you want more children in your classes then you need to be marketing to their parents. If you are trying to attract single professional adults then your marketing should reflect the same professionalism they expect.

I don't like to train fighters, so we don't mention competition on our website. It doesn't mean that I won't ever train a fighter, but it does mean that I'm not trying to attract them with my initial marketing message. If I do receive a call from someone that wants to fight I tell from the beginning that we don't really specialise in that. It makes it easier communicating that from the start than having to explain it at a later date.

If you get your marketing right you will attract the right type of people for you and your school. You will be happy, they will be happy and they will stay longer, thus increasing your retention.

Now list all the things you know about your ideal student. It may be one that already exists in your school, or maybe you haven't met them yet. Write it all down, don't leave out any of the details. The more you can get to know your ideal student the easier it will be to create the correct marketing message.

Here are some things to get you started:

Age :

Gender :

Interests :

Job :

Family :

Hobbies :

Attitude :

Where do they hang out :

What do they want from martial arts training :

PRE-FRAMING PROSPECTS TO BECOME LIFELONG STUDENTS

When you make first contact with your new ideal prospect its important to explain your training philosophy and time-frames. This will help them build realistic expectations if they continue to train with you.

We live in a society where everything can be purchased instantly and many people expect the same when it comes to martial arts training. We know as long term martial art practitioners, that is not the case. To learn any worthwhile skill takes time and dedication. Learning martial arts is no different and it's important to re-enforce that concept when you are speaking to new students. Explain that studying martial arts is a lifelong endeavour. Take them through your grading system and explain how long everything takes. Prepare them for the long road ahead.

ENCOURAGING PROSPECTS TO TURN UP TO THEIR TRIAL CLASS

Of course none of this "retention stuff" matters if the student doesn't turn up to their trial class. Here's a great tip to encourage prospects to turn up to their trial class. I always end my calls to new prospects with the following sentence:

"Please let me know if you can't make your trial, so we can offer your space to someone else"

This makes sure they turn up for their trial class because their space will be offered to someone else. No one likes to lose their spot to someone else. This reduces no-shows significantly.

Try it and let me know how it impacts your school.

THE IMPORTANCE OF A PAR - Q & INFORMATION FORM

Once the new prospect arrives at your school for a trial you should give them a PAR-Q form. A PAR-Q form is a questionnaire that helps to establish if a new student is ready to start classes. It will give you essential information about any health issues they may have, temporary or permanent. It's also a perfect opportunity to record more information about your prospect and their reasons for starting, how they found out about your school, and if they have any specific goals they want to achieve.

Finding out this information at the beginning of their first session will help you to make their first session specific to their goals, which will make them more likely to join. For example, if a person mentions "self-defence" on their PAR-Q then you could add more self-defence drills to that class.

Your PAR-Q form is also a great way of breaking the ice when they arrive at your school for the first time. It gives them a task to do the moment they arrive and they are less likely to get nervous about what might be going on around them. Ideally, you will have someone manning your reception that can do that for you. It may be one of your students, your partner or someone you employ, depending on the size of your school.

Whoever you choose for this position, regardless of their grade, needs to be confident, comfortable talking to new people, and also understand the systems of your school. Chances are they will be asked questions, so you will want them to answer confidently.

USING NLP TO CREATE RAPPORT WITH NEW STUDENTS

Another worthwhile tool to use when greeting any of your students, especially new ones, is NLP (Neuro-linguistic programming). NLP allows you to create rapport with the person you are greeting as quickly as possible. You do this by seamlessly matching their body language and tone of voice. For example, if a quiet person shuffles through your doors, nervous and unsure, it's no good approaching them with a big hug and hard slap on their back. This would probably intimidate them. In this situation, I would use a more gentle greeting. Try to match the person's communication style.

NLP works because "we all like people who are like us" so making an effort to match a new students "style of communication" will make them feel more relaxed and comfortable. I like to match body posture and tone of voice but there are many other things you can match. Do some research on NLP and communication online to find out more.

Learning NLP is an advanced skill, but when you start getting it right you will quickly notice the different personalities in your school and that will help you put them at ease. A person who is comfortable and at ease is more likely to stick around for longer.

THE SIX HUMAN NEEDS & MARTIAL ARTS

We are going to continue on this psychological theme and go a little deeper. Tony Robbins the famous Success Coach notes that there are six fundamental emotional needs:

1. The need for certainty
2. The need for uncertainty
3. The need for significance
4. The need for connection
5. The need for growth
6. The need for contribution

These are needs that all humans want to get met. You'll want to use all of these in your martial arts school, consistently, all of the time. Once you get these right retention sky rockets.

1. Certainty :

Martial arts gives people certainty, through self-confidence, fitness, belief and structure. You'll also want to create certainty within your teaching and your syllabus. Students want to know where they are going, what their objectives are, what's the next step and when is their next grading.

2. Uncertainty :

Too much certainty can get boring and predictable. So we add uncertainty by adding variety to our classes. Switch things up regularly and update your syllabus as needed so that it becomes interesting and challenging without feeling unattainable. Change who teaches a class or invite a guest instructor now and then. Uncertainty creates excitement

3. Significance :

Your students need to feel valued and significant. You do this by building relationships with your students and taking the time to chat with each of them about their goals, hopes and fears. Belt gradings also make students feel significant, so schedule regular gradings.

The simplest and easiest way to make a person feel significant is to praise them publicly for something they did well. We all like to be praised in public so catch a student doing something well and put the spotlight on them in front of their peers.

4. Connection :

Students need to feel connected to your school and the teachers. Create a "family" or "tribal" feel to your school. Everyone should be looking after each other. Instructors should push students to become the best versions of themselves whilst offering support and guidance. Encourage students to connect with each other by hosting regular social events.

5. Growth :

All your students need to feel that they are improving and taking steps closer to their next goal. Every couple of months they need to notice changes in their body and techniques to feel better about themselves. No one likes to feel stagnant, so make sure your students are growing physically, mentally and socially.

6. Contribution :

Naturally, over time, your students will want to give back. That maybe by helping other students within their training session. It could be that they help clean the mats at the end of the session, or give your school a new lick of paint when needed, or it might mean a bigger commitment by becoming a teacher. Regardless of what it is, big or small, most people feel the need to contribute and its important that you create opportunities for your students to fulfil this need.

Hopefully, you can see how the six human needs apply to your martial arts school. Use them to guide your decisions when it comes to students and you won't go wrong.

MENTORING

Mentoring is where an intermediate student takes a beginner under their wing and helps them out for the first few months. This is a great confidence booster to a new student who, maybe, doesn't know anyone yet. Its also great for your midrange student who will be given responsibility to help guide a new student (significance

& contribution). This will also set them on the road to becoming a teacher further down the line.

I don't usually ask black belts to be mentors. Black belts, in general, don't like training with beginners. It's frustrating for your black belt level students and could be intimidating to your new students if their partner doesn't have the patience to help them. I prefer to use students who have trained for one to two years as mentors as they still remember what it's like to be a beginner and feel empathy for them.

The period that a new student is mentored could be over one or two months. You would need to see what works for your school. In return, once those new students graduate to be your mid range students, they will, in turn, become mentors to new students. They will want to give back as they will remember the investment that others made in them and how helpful and reassuring it was to have support in the beginning.

Not all of your students will want to be mentors. It's best to ask who would like to be involved and see who comes forward. You could do this via your Facebook group/ page or ask at the end of your class. There is no point trying to force someone to do this as it will only cause friction that will ultimately affect the student they are mentoring.

SPEND TIME WITH YOUR STUDENTS

It's important as the Chief Instructor that you spend time with new students. I'm not suggesting that you start meeting them down the pub after every class. But it is important that you can take a couple of minutes each week to be personal with them. Call them by their name, and check in with them to see how they are getting on. Ask for any feedback they would like to share.

The only caution I would raise at this point is that you will have students that can talk for hours and will want all your attention. Set a limit on your "face time" so that you can create a meaningful relationship with each of your students, not just the chatter boxes.

SET A GRADING DATE AS SOON AS POSSIBLE

Try to set a grading date within a few weeks of a new student joining. This will give them their first real goal to aim for. Their grading might not be for another 3 or 4 months, but it will be clear what they are training towards and how much time they have to get there. It's also a great way to encourage your C grade students to turn up to class more regularly. Students working towards a clearly defined goal are less likely to quit.

3 POINTS OF CONTACT

Try to have three points of contact with each student during each class. That can be as simple as using their name, or their nickname three times. It could also be through complimenting them when they do well or helping them with a tricky technique. Physical touch can be used but is a sensitive subject. Sometimes it's necessary to physically move your students when teaching, but you certainly don't want to be doing it inappropriately.

A simple way to do this is to only touch bones. You never want to be touching anything soft. If you have to move a student or adjust their position only touch bony parts like their elbow, wrist or knee. A subtle way to touch is with a high five at the end of your class (great for kids) or the occasional shoulder tap. These are very casual and accepted forms of appreciation. The more you are actively engaged with your students the more likely they are to stick around.

(I have a referral offer to encourage my students to refer their friends to my school. When their friend signs up I give them £25 and a hug. Amazingly they always ask for the hug first before the cash. So it proves that some physical contact is desired from your students and everyone likes to be thanked. Find different ways to show appreciation for your students.)

GET THEM TO INVEST IN EQUIPMENT

Equipment is a great way to increase someone's commitment to your classes as well creating profit for your school. When your students invest their hard earned cash into equipment they are much more likely to continue training. Most gyms have spare gloves and pads that people are welcome to use, but at some point, you want to get them to invest in their own. Our gloves and pads are used so often they do smell a bit. There is not much we can do about it, but it's another good reason for them to buy their own. It's not a nice feeling putting your hands into a pre-sweated glove.

I make up basic kit packs for people to purchase. It will include all of their basic equipment to get them started. It makes it easy for them to buy their equipment all in one go and it will also be less stress for you selling bundles of equipment rather than separate items. Your pack could include a kit bag, gloves, gum shields and focus mitts. You could then create an another pack for sparring which includes; shin guards, groin guard and hand wraps. It's possible to create different equipment packs to suit the classes within your school.

2, 4 & 6 WEEKS FOLLOW UP CALLS

Do you schedule two, four and six weekly follow up calls with your new students? These calls are the perfect time to start a casual conversation to how they are settling in and find out if there are any concerns they may have. Maybe they need a little extra help with their stretching, you could, at this point, send them a video on stretching or offer them a 15 minute private to give them some pointers. Follow up calls show your new students that you care about their progress. This will boost retention massively.

Think about who will be responsible for these follow-up calls. Your instructors or staff will have different personalities that will match well with certain characters. So find the right person to make the follow-up calls. Someone upbeat and enthusiastic usually works best.

Try to call all new students after 2, 4 & 6 weeks training.

THE TLC PROGRAM

The Tender Loving Care (TLC) program is a 100-day system that will show your new students how much you care about their experience at your school. How do you create a TLC program? You need to make a list of 100 things that you can do to make your new student feel cared for and appreciated and do one each day. Think about absolutely everything you can do to make your student feel valued.

If you look after them for the first 100 days, (which is the dreaded danger zone), they are more likely to stick around for a long time.

Let's look at some examples of what could be on your TLC list. Your list will be individual to you, but these ideas will suit most schools :

- A reminder text for their first trial class
- A warm personal welcome on their first visit to your school
- Mentoring during their first month with an existing student
- Educational weekly emails to support their training and goals
- A beginners website or FB group that will help to answer frequently asked questions

- Inviting them to join your school's Facebook group
- Free grading seminars (so they feel more confident to grade)
- Free 15 minute privates (as needed)
- Mat chats, (relaxed conversations on the mat about how they are doing)
- Remembering their birthday, send them a text or a card
- Student of the month or ninja of the week (great for kids)
- 2, 4 & 6 - week calls
- Missing in action calls, when you don't see them for a week
- Training tips, via mat chats or automated emails
- Thank your students, publicly in front of their peers
- Call them by their name or nickname
- Recognise your top referrers. Give them something in return for their support
- Give out free Tshirt's to new students (consider it a marketing expense)
- Really listen to your students when they come to talk to you
- Create special clubs in your school: black belt clubs, demo club, masters club, etc.

Everyone likes to be part of something and it gives them something to aspire to

This is just a small example of some of the things that could be included in your TLC list. Ultimately it has to work for you so I'm not going to write this list for you, but hopefully, there are enough prompts within this book and the list above that will help get you started.

It's worth investing your time to create this list as it will make your school far more successful in the long run. It will also change as your school and students evolve. It's not set in stone, so if there is something that doesn't work then you can take it out, tweak it or change it for something else.

When a student feels valued they are far more likely to talk to others how much they enjoy their time at your school. This is a great time to ask them to be included in video tutorials or testimonials. It's surprising how many people like to see themselves in a video and you can use the footage in your marketing.

SEND HELPFUL EMAILS TO SUPPORT THEIR FIRST 100 DAYS

It's worth taking the time to write a series of welcome emails to send to new members of your school. Once they are written you will then be able to use these emails over and over again. Once you have completed 10-20 TLC emails, you can then send them out to 1000's of new students automatically without any extra work.

The subject of these emails can be as varied as you like, from a general welcome to more specific support for their training. This will be entirely up to you and the type of support your students need.

They can include subjects like:

- Welcome to the school...
- What to expect in the first 30 days...
- How do gradings work?...
- How to deal with an injury...
- Overcoming muscle soreness...
- How to stretch...
- How to use hand wraps...
- How to spar safely...
- The story of our school...
- Diet and nutrition tips

You can see how easy it is to start writing a list of email subjects. Just think of the questions you get asked most by beginners to get you started. Then you need to take the time sit down and write them. Once you have these written you can use the likes of Mailchimp or another email provider that will automate the delivery of these emails to your list of students as and when they join.

The other advantage of using a tool like Mailchimp is that reporting is instant and really easy. This means you will be able to study the behaviour of your students to see if they are opening all, some or none of your emails. You will be able to see if some email subjects are more successful than others.

PRAISE

We mentioned praise on the TLC list. Numerous research studies about praise in the workplace have shown that it's worth more than money to an employee. Especially if it is done publicly so that their community can see. Praise will go a long way in your school. It doesn't mean that you have to be giving it to every student at every session, find your flow and figure out what feels comfortable to you. I make it a habit to publicly praise at least three students in every class I teach. Ask yourself are you more or less likely to quit if you've just been praised in front of all your friends?

ASK FOR STUDENT FEEDBACK

We are there to serve our students so it makes sense that we listen to what they have to say. If you ask your students outright if there are any problems, most of them won't give you an honest answer, because no one likes to upset a person that they respect.

There are a couple of ways that you can combat this. Firstly you could have some 'spies' within your school who will be your eyes and ears and report back to you if they hear of anything negative. These spies could be your intermediate students, your instructors or other staff within the school that are likely to hear or see things you might miss on a regular basis.

Another way is to share an online survey where you post the questions and students can give feedback anonymously. I like to use www.typeform.com for this. Their free survey tool looks great and is simple to use. Once its set up you can text or email the link to your students. Questions you might ask include:

- How do you find training our school?
- What do you enjoy most?
- What do you like least?
- Is there something you would like us to improve?
- How do you rate our classes on a scale of 1 - 10?
- How would you describe your experience at our school?

If you feel that your students might need a little more motivation to give you the feedback you could enter them into a prize draw to win some new equipment. Of course, this would only work if they are happy to give you their details.

If you don't think your students will visit your online survey, you can print copies and have them available in your reception so that you can give them to everyone that attends your classes that week. Whatever questions you choose make sure they are open questions (not yes or no answers) and that it's short and snappy and can be completed in less than 2-3 minutes. Any longer and they will most likely get bored and not give you very useful answers. I can honestly say a survey is one of the best things that I have done in my school.

Having this open feedback will help to eliminate gripes and issues that will arise in your school. It will also give you a chance to address these issues without them getting out of control. You will always learn something new about the needs and expectations of your students every time you survey them.

CREATE SEPARATE FACEBOOK GROUPS

Facebook is not for everyone. If you don't like social media, skip this tip or get one of your teenage students to set you up and coach you on the magic of social media. If you like to use Facebook daily, then Facebook groups can be a very effective (and free) way of managing how you communicate with your existing students.

Setting up separate Facebook groups is an effective way to share specific information to different groups in your school. I recommend having at least three separate groups, a student group, a parents group, and a fighters group. This allows you to share specific information that is relevant to a particular section within your school. This means each group gets the information and support they specifically need. Plus, it's another way of making your students feel special and cared for.

SHARING OTHER PEOPLES CONTENT TO HELP YOUR STUDENTS

You can also use your Facebook pages and groups to share other people's content. Why would you want to do that? Well, there is lots of amazing information out there that would be really useful to your students. So do the right thing and share it with your students. It's also a great time saver for you, borrowing content from different places will add variety and diversity to your page, making it more interesting. There is no point trying to redesign the wheel, just ensure that the content works in line with your martial arts school brand and ethics.

If it moves you there is a great chance that it will also move your students. It's important to remember that you cannot do everything and be amazing at everything, so if someone is doing something that you like and is relevant to your students then share it on your social media pages, whether its a video or an article. Your students will appreciate you sharing useful content and this will keep them coming back for more.

SPECIAL UNIFORM

Most schools will have a standard uniform that all students need to wear when training. It's worth creating unique uniforms for special groups within your school. For example, our teenage "class helpers" have a special T-shirt that distinguishes them from the other students. This makes them feel special and unique. And that boosts retention.

You could have a special T-shirt for your demo team, your fight team or your elite black belts.

DEMO TEAMS

Speaking of teams, do you have a demo team in your school? Demo teams are a great way to create exposure for your school at different events in your local area. One word of warning, demo teams can be time-consuming to set up and maintain. But if you have a small group of students that are keen to show off their skills, it could well be worth your while setting one up. It will give those students a platform to perform on and generate new leads for your school. Plus everyone who is a member of your demo team feels excited and special which helps them stay longer.

FIGHT TEAMS

Fight teams are different from your demo teams. Members of the demo teams are those that like to show off their skills. Your fight team will consist of those that genuinely want to fight (or those that think they want to fight). You will need a selection process to help you find out those that really want to fight, from those that romanticise about being a fighter, (which is probably 90% of your school.)

I would set the stage and let them know that there will be try-outs for your school's fight team starting on a certain date. As a prerequisite, they will need to be training a minimum of three days a week and attend one sparring class a week. This will help to make the first phase of cuts. Those that can't manage that commitment, can't try out for the fight team.

The other cuts will occur when you run your fight team try-outs. Make the try-out process tough and challenging, not everyone should get through. It should include physical and technical elements and push people to their limits (but never over). If their goal is to be on the fight team they will go the extra mile in preparation, which is great for your school's retention.

SHARE MOTIVATIONAL MATERIAL

From time to time I like to give away free motivational posters. They are affordable and something that your students will look at frequently. Not only will you be motivating them, but it will also be a constant reminder of your school.

These free posters work well for both adults and children across all levels and abilities.

CREATE A TOP HEAVY SYLLABUS

The perfect martial arts syllabus is a pyramid turned on its head. Your white belts are at the bottom, the point of the pyramid, and your black belts are at the widest part, at the top. Its common for martial arts teachers to create their syllabus the other way round, a bottom heavy syllabus. A bottom heavy syllabus is where you will have a long list of requirements for your white belts and slowly reducing the list of requirements until they get their black belt.

This, as you can imagine is stressful for your beginners. Not only will they be attending their first grading, but you will be giving them a long list of things to remember for their first belt. This makes the whole thought of grading unpleasant.

I recommend doing the opposite. Make their first grading simple and easy. That way you've set them up to look forward to gradings. In my school, for their first belt grading, students are required to do only four things plus some basic fitness drills. On completing these requirements they pass.

This supports your new students, motivates them to continue their training and reduces the amount of stress, which if too demanding, is a great reason to quit your school. I'm not concerned with making great yellow belts, I just want fantastic black belts. So my focus is on getting new students comfortable with grading and gradually increasing the intensity over each grade.

When you are preparing and writing your syllabus (which of course will develop, change and evolve over time), think about what you want to teach after black belt. You don't want to make the gradings up to black belt too complex and then have nothing left to show them once they earn their black belt. After black belt is where all the learning is supposed to happen. Up until that point, they have been building a strong base of good technique. At black belt, everything should switch up a gear. If you don't think about what to teach after black belt you will have a school full of black belts that will drop out as they get bored training the same things over and over again.

USE A CHARACTER EDUCATION PROGRAM

Parents do want their kids to get the fitness and self-defence benefits of the martial arts but they also want their children to learn about self-esteem, how to deal with bullying, peer pressure, confidence, respect etc. So do you have a character education program in place to teach this material at your school? If you don't, its something that I recommend that you develop as soon as possible because its what many parents want for their children. You, therefore, need to show them how their kids are also learning these character skills as well as kicking and punching. If you are unsure where to start, check out Mike Massie's great book called :

Martial Arts Character Education Lesson Plans for Children

If you would like to offer a program specifically on tackling bullying, look no further than Dave Kovar. He has created an excellent anti-bullying program in the United States and gives open access to his course on his website for everyone to use.

Download his course adjust the wording or presentation to suit your school's culture.

His website is www.donewithbullying.com

GRADINGS BOOST RETENTION

Gradings boost retention by offering short term goals and rewarding consistent attendance. Make sure your students are aware that in order to be eligible to grade they must attend a certain amount of classes. This makes sure they show up to class and learn the syllabus.

People who don't grade tend to quit because they have no short or long term goals keeping them moving forward. 97% of my school grades every four months. Encourage all your students to grade.

FAMILY DISCOUNTS

You will have your regular grading prices but, do you offer family discounts? Normally we charge the first two family members at full price and then discount those thereafter. It will help to make gradings affordable for families and encourage them to progress through your syllabus.

CATCH - UP GRADINGS

My school also offers catch-up gradings and private gradings. It's not possible to set a grading date that will be suitable for every member of your school, so don't try to. There are many reasons why students may have missed their grading; maybe they were unwell, injured, or on holiday. We host a catch-up grading a month after the main grading and it enables us to serve most if not all of our students. Typically 80% of our students attend our main grading and the other 20% make the catch-up grading.

Private gradings are slightly different. You will set a time which works for both yourself and your student. As they are paying for a one on one privilege you cannot charge the same price as you would for the regular grading (or everyone will want to do it). We add £30-50 to the price of our regular gradings for a private grading. So if your group grading was priced at £30 then your private grading would be £60-80. But, you can, of course, charge any price you see fit.

We structure our private gradings along the same lines as the regular gradings. We start with a welcome, set the expectations and then straight into a vigorous warm up. We like to get them doing skipping, press ups, sit ups and squats for time. We'll have a short water break and move them onto the bag, working on their grading combinations. Next, we move onto the pads where we continue the techniques but also add in defences and footwork. Finally, we like to finish with some sparring to see the techniques applied against a resisting partner.

BOOST RETENTION BY CREATING AN ONLINE MARTIAL ARTS SCHOOL

Having an online school boosts retention. This is because your online school is always open, never gets ill or takes holidays. This means students can get access to training material whenever they need it. And these days its very easy to build a simple online training website that contains videos and downloads that will help support your student's training when they are not in class.

You can use video platforms like Vimeo or YouTube and create private groups for your students only. Or you can use WIX (a free website building tool) to create your online school. It's very easy to use and you can build a website with a members section within a few hours. Think of it as an online university where you students can go to get more information about techniques or subjects to support their training. Offering an online school along with your physical school encourages your students to keep training for longer.

(The other great thing these online tools is that your students will be able to access them on their mobile devices. The majority of what is viewed on the web nowadays is viewed on a smartphone or a tablet. The likes of WIX will create a mobile friendly website for you, without you having to do any extra work. Vimeo and Youtube are both experts at delivering content to mobile devices so there is nothing extra that you will need to do to ensure you tick those boxes.)

Think about all of the information that you have already made for your students, whether as a handout or via email. All of these will help to build the resources for your online school. It's possible to recycle a lot of the work you have already done and it will be accessible for all the new students coming to your school when they sign up.

Once your content is live, it's live forever, unless you take it down of course to make updates. There's an investment of time in the beginning but it will pay you back by keeping students with you for the longer.

OFFER HOME TRAINING ROUTINES

Create home training routines, so that when your students can't make it to class they can train at home. Keep it simple with minimal or no equipment. Simplicity is key. If it's too technical they will probably just watch it and not do it. You could include sprints, push ups, sit ups, mountain climbers, shadow-boxing, skipping, squats, planking variations, the list is endless. This gives students who maybe missed a lesson through no fault of their own (like bad traffic) the chance to do something productive and keeps them in the training mindset.

THE MARTIAL ARTS INSTRUCTORS DILEMMA

One of the biggest problems with martial arts business is you trade time for money. That is, you teach a class and get paid for your time. If you want to earn more money, you need to have more students or teach more classes. Believe me after 15 years that becomes tiring and is not really sustainable as a business model on its own. You will be constantly giving, sharing and pushing out your energy to your students with a limited cap on how much you can earn.

To increase the stability of your business it's important to look at other ways to earn money that doesn't require you to physically be there.

In my case I created mittmaster.com. A website that delivers training videos specialising in pad training and techniques. It's a product that has become a passive income source that supports my business and my family.

Here's how it works. Basically, I film some material, I upload it to the web, I tell people about it and they buy it. Once it's done it I can continue to sell it forever. It requires no more time or energy from me. I only need to make that content once to gain multiple sales from one product.

Selling martial arts training online means you will no longer be trading time for money. Once your product is live you won't need to touch to it again. It's there working for you on the internet 24/7, 365.

If you would like more information about how to create and sell martial arts products online please go to : www.teachyourpassiononline.co.uk

HOST EXTRA CURRICULAR SEMINARS

We like to host seminars on subjects that we don't normally cover in classes. This is a great opportunity to invite some guest instructors to your school to teach your students. It creates variety and excitement that will both motivate and educate your students and in turn benefit them in their regular training.

We have invited Yoga Instructors, Jiu Jitsu Instructors and Massage Practitioners to host one-off seminars. Often the content they are teaching may be a subject that you have been banging on about for an ages, (like the importance of stretching), but because it's a guest instructor they haven't met before they will pay more attention. When hosting one of these seminars, ensure that you have enough lead time to market your event (typically six weeks), set a minimum and maximum attendance limit that you need to be able to run the event.

Knowing your minimum numbers will ensure that the seminar is cost effective and you are not paying out of your own pocket if people don't book. Setting a maximum number is something that you can do to create a sense of urgency so that students sign up quickly to reserve their place.

In addition to one-off seminars, you can also create short courses that will run over a set period of time (typically 4 to 6 weeks). I've run a stretching and kicking course. A wrestling for MMA course. A kid's nun-chuck course and so on. Set the price and work out how many people you need to sign up to make the course profitable and market it until you have at least that number.

As well as teaching a seminar or course you can also film the event and then sell it online afterwards. I recently hosted a sparring seminar at my school. I had around 25 attendees and they each paid me £20 for the seminar. I filmed the entire seminar, did some basic editing and uploaded my seminar to my product website. I am now selling that video online and am able to reach a larger audience than my seminar ever could. As we mentioned before, once the content is online it will continue to sell for the foreseeable future, earning you money forever.

In regards to guest instructors, I clearly tell them that I plan to film their seminar and that it will be edited and sold online. Once the video is edited I give the guest instructor a copy for them to use as they please. They can sell it or use it as promotional material, its up to them. I upload my video to my website www.mittmaster.com and start marketing and selling it online.

If you are honest and upfront about your intentions then your guest instructors will be happy to accommodate your requests. Not only are they being paid for their seminar, but they will also walk away with a product that they can sell themselves.

You can also swap with your guest instructors. They come to your school to give a seminar and you return the favour and give a seminar at their school. Guest instructors will keep your students excited which will increase the retention at your school. If you create enough variety within your school your students are less likely to look elsewhere for inspiration.

HOST OUTDOOR TRAINING

In the summer months, we like to take some training outside. We create some cool boot camp style courses. We are covering pretty much the same training as we do inside the dojo but we are taking it outside. People feel different outside, it brings a different atmosphere to their training and also has a long list of health benefits. One thing to keep in mind about public spaces is that they can be monitored (by local councils) for certain activities and you may be asked to move on. It's worth having a look around your area and discover where you will be welcome to host these types of training sessions without getting into the red tape of applying for event permission.

RE-ACTIVATING EX-STUDENTS

It's worth taking some time to plan how we can re-activate our old students who have stopped training for one reason or another. These ex-students will be easier to re-sign than generating new leads and converting new prospects. They already understand how you work and what your classes are like, but maybe they just got out of the habit if training. You could start by giving them a call, sending them an email or a text message or even post on your social media pages inviting them back. At my school, November is normally our welcome back month. We want to welcome back our old students before we get an influx of new students at the start of the following year.

Our welcome back offer message will be somewhere along the lines of "We miss you. Come back and get one month's free training and a free t-shirt". Many people that quit your school would like to get back to training again it's just that life got in the way. Take the time to contact them and invite them back.

Each time we do this we get four or five old students back to class. It increases their lifetime value and you don't need to spend time introducing them to the way you work. They already get you and your school. It's a very cost and time effective marketing activity.

CELEBRATE FIRSTS

There will be many "firsts" for your students along their martial arts path. It's important that you recognise these firsts and help celebrate them. The first time you do something has special significance for most people so use this to your advantage.

Here are some ideas:

- Celebrate them completing their first class
- Celebrate them passing their first grading
- Celebrate the first time the refer a new member
- Celebrate their first year of training
- Celebrate their black belt achievement

What other firsts could you celebrate?

Celebrate firsts, it makes your students feel valued and will motivate them onto their next goal, increasing their value as a student for you and your business.

CONCLUSION

We have touched on many ways to help increase student retention within this book. Some of these ideas you might already be doing but try to tweak them to make them more efficient. Some ideas might be brand new to you. The key as with everything is to start! Set yourself an action plan and start putting things into practice, and you will start seeing the results.

Meet with other school owners and brainstorm retention ideas. Getting together with other people who are facing the same problems and coming up with their own solutions is both inspiring and educational. So get together with a few martial arts friends and chat about what retention strategies are working for each of you. I guarantee you will come away with a few new ideas you can try.

It doesn't end here though. Business is a life work. You will need to continue to educate yourself and find out about new ideas and approaches. Google the latest retention strategies. You'll find more there than you will ever need to know and it's mostly free. It may seem strange that I have written this book and now I am telling you to go and find all of this information online, but we know that the internet can be a big and confusing place. My aim with this book is to give you the grounding and confidence to continue your research on retention so you will be able to build a bigger and stronger business that will support you and your family.

Now you understand the basics of retention, the information you find online will become less intimidating, it will make more sense and you'll be able to put it to better use. Continue to invest in your education and learning.

Go back through the book and make notes. Highlight those ideas that will work for you. It should be something that you refer to over and over again (so put this book by your toilet if you need to). Read it through once and then use it as a reference manual, your business and students will thank you for it.

MARTIAL ARTISTS GUIDE TO WRITING BETTER COPY

WHAT IS COPYWRITING?

Wikipedia defines Copywriting as "the act of writing text for the purpose of advertising or other forms of marketing" .

I prefer to think of copywriting as using written words to persuade a person to take a particular action. That's what we all want. We want people to read our copy and click the button to buy the course or book the lesson.

Good copywriting helps people take action.

Apart from this primary goal copywriting also has several other functions. Firstly, original copy helps to make the website stand out from the millions of other sites that are already up and running. Even if the subject matter is the same that is found elsewhere, original copy is your chance to put your own personality and experience out there.

Along with making the site stand out a little more, creating original copy also makes it possible to use targeted keywords to your advantage. This can also help to push your sites ranking up a few more notches in search engines.

Strategically placing keywords will help to improve the chances of showing up in search engine results and higher rankings means more visitors. If the purpose of the site is to market a product or service, this is a very good thing.

Lastly, copywriting provides a creative outlet. Drafting original content makes it possible to show the world what you have to offer in the way of new ideas, style, concepts and opinions.

UNDERSTANDING YOUR CUSTOMER

The single most important thing in copywriting is understanding your customer. If you don't fully know your customer (their wants, fears, desires, problems and pain) your copy will miss the mark and you won't get the sale.

Understanding your customer is the most important step in copywriting.

How do you understand your customers?

Well it definitely helps if you are your customer. I create online courses for martial arts instructors and I've been an instructor myself for over 25 years! I really understand how they think and feel because I'm fighting the same daily battles with them.

To start this process of understanding your customer, start with yourself.

Answer these questions:

- Your name.
- Your age.
- Your gender.
- Your occupation.
- Your interests.
- Your fears.
- Your daily routine.
- Obstacles that stop you.
- Frustrations that drive you mad.
- Your passions.
- Your hopes for the future.

Now do the same for your ideal clients (if you have some). For me my ideal clients are full time martial arts instructors who see the benefit of online training and spend at least £200 per year on online courses.

When I looked through my customer database one instructor stood out.

INTRODUCING FORREST

Forrest found some of my videos on YouTube, He liked and commented on several. He then went to my Facebook page and became a fan.

He bought a few of my cheaper online courses. Then bought everything else (nearly £1500 of online content).

He completed my online instructor certification. Then flew to the UK, from America, to train personally with me.

He constantly recommends me to others and helps me generate sales and goodwill in the USA. He is also an affiliate and sells Mittmaster programmes for a 50% commission.
Who is your Forrest?

Use the next section to map out your ideal client. Once you fully understand them All your copy should be focused on helping them.

You are not trying to sell to everyone, just your ideal customer.

- Name
- Age
- Gender
- Occupation
- Interests
- Fears
- Daily problems
- Obstacles that stop them
- Frustrations that drive them mad
- Passions

THE SIX P'S OF COPYWRITING

Now that you know who your ideal customer is it's time to introduce the Six P's of copywriting. Using this simple formula will make all the difference in how your copy performs.

Here are each of the Six P's along with a simple definition.

Problem – Whenever your task is to convince someone to buy your product or service, you must first convince the buyer there is a problem that must be addressed. This problem helps to set up a sense of urgency, indicating action must be taken in order to take care of the issue at hand. Once your copy presents this problem, then you can begin the process of convincing the buyer you have the solution.

Pain – Once the reader is aware of the problem you need to amplify the pain if they do nothing. You need to take them on a journey from where they are now into the future where the pain becomes unbearable.

Promise – Amplifying the pain makes your prospect uncomfortable and helps them take action. Your promise is that your product or service is going to make everything okay again.

Proof – Having made a promise or claim, it is now time to put your money where your mouth is. In other words, you are going to present all the reasons why your solution works better than anything else. Here is where you make your solution irresistible to your ideal client by providing testimonials and reviews

Price – After making all the benefits clear, you can start to introduce how much your solution costs. The idea here is to convey that your solution is worth every penny of the cost, even if it may be a little more than some of the similar but obviously inferior products offered by the competition.

P.S. – This is where you summarise the awesome opportunity you are presenting and is your final chance to nudge a prospect who is on the fence to go ahead and take the plunge.

This simple formula can be utilised with just about any type of situation where you want to present a product or service and then offer a viable solution. You can use it on websites, sales pages, emails and social media adverts. It works everywhere.

Don't expect to become a master copywriter on your first attempt. You have to give it time and practice. Just like martial arts, the more you practice the better you get.

NOTES:

HOW TO WRITE A COMPELLING HEADLINE THAT QUALIFIES YOUR IDEAL CUSTOMER

No matter how well crafted the body of your copy is, a headline that grabs attention will always make a difference. Of course, you want to grab the right kind of attention. You want your ideal target reader to be attracted by the headline and thus want to read the body of the text.

Here are three simple tips to keep your headlines interesting, compelling, and attractive to your audience.

Tip # 1 – Keep it simple, stupid. Yes, the old KISS principle. When it comes to your headline, don't get too excited with the word count. Choose your words carefully and use no more than you need to grab attention. A headline is not meant to tell the whole story. It should help your prospect know what is coming next and encourage them to read the next line.

Tip # 2 – Make it relevant. Headlines need to speak to a specific problem or pain the reader is currently experiencing. The headline should arouse curiosity. The reader feels compelled to continue.

One of the best headline/video title I've written was about setting up punches to the body in boxing. I had a few ideas, but all my headlines felt bland like "How to punch the body in boxing"

Booooooring.

After a lot of thought I came up with "Discover The Most Painful Punch In Boxing" (which in case you didn't know is the liver punch).

That is a great headline. It's interesting, increases curiosity and compels you to continue reading.

Tip # 3 – Make the headline memorable. You want people to recommend the content to other people. If the headline is so bland that it really doesn't stick, then you will lose a lot of attention. While you want simplicity and relevance, you do not want boring. Make the headline zippy and something people will want to share.

Headlines are often overlooked as being unimportant or just a formulaic construct of writing copy. Neither concept is true. Headlines are essential and can play a huge role in grabbing attention. When coupled with compelling copy, a great headline can make all the difference between success and failure.

THE SLIPPERY SLOPE PRINCIPLE

So you have edited and re-edited and you have a cracking headline.

What next?

You want your reader to read through all of your copy.
You want them to make it to the end as that is where they decide to make a purchase and you take one step closer to hitting your next target.

You want them to hit the buy button!

The slippery slope principle is how you will hold your readers hand and lead them down the slope. You will intentionally design your copy to lead them from section to the next finally landing on that buy now button.

Your headline should draw them in. It should grab their attention and leave them wanting more. Your slippery slope will then lead them onto the sub-title. Which will wet their appetite.

You've got them, but they are not there yet.

Each step should gift a piece of the puzzle, but equally leave wanting more.
Each headline and paragraph will lead them to the next and finally arrive at the call to action destination.

THINGS TO CONSIDER WHEN YOU ARE REVIEWING YOUR COPY:

- Does one section flow into the next?
- Is it simple, clear and direct?
- Does each section point to the call to action?
- Does each section relate to the one before, without unnecessary repetition?
- Is it relevant?
- Have someone else read it. Listen to their feedback.

THE COMPELLING STORY TECHNIQUE

Any successful copy is going to tell a story. Just how well that story is told makes all the difference in whether or not a prospect turns into a customer. Here are a few tips to help you tell your story in a way that will hold the attention of the prospect and keeps it all the way through to the close of the sale.

Set the stage for your story. The idea is to grab the interest of the reader by presenting a situation / problem or pain that he or she can relate to. Ideally, the situation will form the basis for your story by creating a conflict that must be resolved. The more your prospect can identify with the conflict, the better your chances of enticing him or her to keep reading.

Offer the ideal solution for taking care of the conflict. In a sense, this is your shining knight that comes over the horizon to save the day. This is your chance to work in all the good qualities that make your solution the perfect way to deal with the conflict and thus restore order to the kingdom, which is the life of your prospect. Use this element to start building confidence that the solution really will work.

TOP TIP: Bulleted lists work well when presenting benefits to the reader and break up text

Demonstrate how the solution does in fact resolve the conflict. You can use case studies, testimonials, or a number of other devices to back up the claims you previously made. Make sure this proof is true and will appeal to your audience in a way that helps them to imagine using the product or service themselves.

Go for the sale. Inspire in the prospect a burning desire to possess this product by recapping all the great things it will do and note how reasonable the cost will be. Once you have established this sense of urgency to own in your prospects, they will quickly become loyal customers who will gladly share your good name far and wide.

Make sure you give a clear call to action that states the benefits of your product or service.

“Click here to get instant access & start using these exciting drills in your class today”.

is better than:

“BUY NOW”.

If you’d like to see these elements in action, click here to see one of my sales pages where I use them: https://mittmaster.thinkific.com/courses/mittmaster-kids-drills

INTRODUCING YOUR OFFER AND INSTILLING THE POWER BENEFITS

In general, your sales copy has only a few seconds to grab the interest of a prospect and move them along to closing the sale. That means you have to provide a quality introduction to what you have to offer and follow it up with all the reasons why your product / service should be chosen above all others.

Here are some simple ideas on how to introduce your offer and quickly instil a sense of urgency about those power benefits.

First, don't spend a lot of time on fancy words.

Write copy in a conversational way, just as if you were speaking to the consumer in person. This will help you to avoid using too many words, and especially to stay away from using too many technical terms that could turn off your prospect. Keep sentences short, simple and easy to read.

Next, focus on the benefits to your ideal customer. Point out the main benefits of the product in question. Relate those benefits to common situations that come along with the problem. Illustrate how those benefits quickly and easily remove obstacles and restore order to chaos. Driving home how your product solves their problems quickly and easily will help to sustain interest and increase the desire to buy.

Third, make sure the reader is aware of what will happen if they do nothing. Remind them of the pain they are in and how it will only get worse if they do nothing!

Fourth, recap the benefits. You can use a summary format for this, perhaps even a bullet list. This helps to reinforce the benefits in the mind of the reader and prepare him or her for the close of the sale.

Lastly, use a strong call to action to help them commit to taking action.

KILLING ALL PROSPECT DOUBTS GETTING THEM ACROSS THE LINE

So your sales copy is great, well written, easy to read and understand… so why is the prospect still hesitating?

Consumers always have objections. It is a fact of life. It is also a fact that you overcame some of them in your copy already. What remains, is to address the rest of them and thus remove all obstacles to the final sale. Here's what you need to do.

Offer a money back guarantee – This will often hook in many consumers who are sitting on the fence. If you are willing to provide a 7, 14 or 30 day money back guarantee you build a lot of trust, confidence and credibility with the prospect.

Create an FAQ to answer common questions – This is your chance to get specific. Use questions that have come up in the past through discussions with established customers or general queries that come via your website or social media. Reading through a well-designed Frequently Asked Questions page can make a huge difference for your prospect. It shows you care and have thought about common questions prospects may have. Plus it saves you time answering these questions via email.

Offer a free trial or discount – this may be a short trial membership (like 7 days), or a discounted offer for new customers. This removes most of the risk for the prospect and will increase the chances of them buying.

Show testimonials from users – Sadly no one trusts you, but they do trust other people who have used your products. Sprinkle your pages with written and video testimonials from happy customers. Social proof is a massive motivator!

Show testimonials from experts – People like to know that some type of expert thinks your product / service is a good choice. Your experts should be respected professionals who have actually used your product and have offered unbiased feedback.

Show it in use – A quick video demo of how your product works can alleviate fears that the product may be too complicated for the prospect to figure out. Calm those fears with a test drive that shows just how user friendly the product really is.

Give bonuses – In other words, provide added value to the benefits already listed. These may be more specific, whereas the earlier content was broad.

ACT NOW - NOT LATER!

One of the goals you have for your sales copy is to compel the reader to make a decision NOW.

All too often, copy builds an excellent case for considering the product, but does not follow through with that little added extra that pushes the prospect off the fence and into making a decision to buy.

Here are a three basic ways to make sure your prospect does not click away, and becomes a devoted customer.

First, don't assume that your prospect remembers all those great advantages you so painstakingly mentioned earlier in your copy. Instead, do a quick recap.

The recap does not have to be an exhaustive replay of all those benefits. In fact, something as simple as a quick bullet-point list will often do the trick.

This simple device makes it possible for the reader to see the benefits one more time without having to scroll backward to review them.

Summarise all the benefits directly before your buy button!

Next use scarcity to create desire.

We all hate missing out on a great deal so use FOMO to help create sales. Scarcity means that whatever you offer is in limited supply and people will need to act NOW to take advantage.

There are three simple ways to use scarcity

1. Limited time. The offer will only be available for a limited time at a lower price. After a cut off date the price will increase significantly. I use this all the time and it works well.
2. Limited quantity. With physical goods this is easier to use as stock will obviously run out at some point. With digital goods it more about giving a small percentage of your customers access to bonuses that will be removed once a certain number of customers have purchased.

Try using something like:

"Only the first 20 customers will get access to bonus never seen before footage of XYZ" works well.

Limited access. Limit the number of customers who can access you and your experience. For example you could run a bonus live workshop where you into depth on a subject related to your product BUT only the first 20 customers can attend.

Getting consumers to buy now is essential. The sad fact is 70-80% of visitors to a website DON'T buy so you need to use these tactics to encourage them to make a decision before they disappear forever.

POWER WORDS

When you need a little inspiration.

Words for newness:
Introducing, welcome, unique, announcing, breakthrough, surprising, exciting, astounding.

Words for exclusivity:
Special, secret, hidden, truth, temptation, forbidden, never, revealed, exclusive, limited.

Words for urgency:
Now, discover, new, results, only, direct, hurry, quick, fast.

Words for reassure:
Can, guarantee, proven, easy, care, simple, safety, lifetime.

Words for saving:
Save, money, win, cheap, free, reduced, bargain, bonus, discount, lowest.

FINAL TIPS AND TRICKS TO IMPROVE YOUR COPY

One thing to keep in mind is there is no such thing as perfect sales copy. There is excellent sales copy that works perfectly today, but there are no guarantees that it will be just as effective a month from now, or even next week. You must continually monitor your copy and see how it performs. If something isn't working as well as it used to try changing the headline first, then test to see if the situation improves.

Of course, there are a few ways you can enhance the effectiveness of your copy and thus extend its life for a bit.

Here are some ideas:

Add video – Make your text come alive with video demo's, face to camera monologues or exciting promos. These can be positioned toward the end of the piece, or strategic points along the way.

Add photos – If video seems like a bit much, then come up with photographs that will help to drive home key points in the flow of the text. These add a bit of visual spice and break up big blocks of text. Best of all, you can change them out with relative ease, and give your content a fresh look from time to time. Always choose photos that show the benefits of your product in action.

Use new fonts – This is so simple that many people overlook it. You can give your text and the entire web page a fresh look simply by making some changes in the font styles and sizes from time to time. Just make sure your choices leave the text easy to read.

Use Google to best advantage – This means inserting strategic keywords in order to drive targeted traffic to the site. Here's a simple guide to some SEO tips that will help:
https://www.bowlerhat.co.uk/seo-tips-beginners

Rework a paragraph here or there – You do not have to completely rewrite the text in order to make it fresh. Changing some wording here and there gives you the chance to add fresh keywords, and also reorders the flow of the text to give it a new feel.

Basically, always be on the lookout for some way to make a good thing better. Consumer tastes and demands change from time to time. With the right touch, you can anticipate those trends and use your copy to stay one step ahead of your competition.

SUMMARY

I hope you enjoyed this short guide to writing better copy. I've deliberately kept it simple so that you can get started right away. I've probably only covered 5% of the tools and tactics used by professional copywriters but that was intentional. My goal was to create a simple guide that will help you get started writing better copy. I hope I have achieved my aim.

If you would like to book a short 15 minute Zoom meeting to discuss your copy or anything else to do with your business please click the link below

matthewchapman.online

Below are some recommended resources that will help you take your copywriting further.

RECOMMENDED RESOURCES

I highly recommend Andrew Holland for copywriting and SEO advice. He is very knowledgeable and really cares about his clients. He can be contacted at: https://zoogly.co.uk/

If you'd like to develop your copywriting skills further the book I most recommend is "How To Write Copy That Sells" by Ray Edwards. It's a great, short book that packs a real punch. Highly recommended!

You can get it here:
https://www.amazon.co.uk/Write-Copy-Sells-Step-Step/dp/161448502X

Also check out this awesome collection of FREE resources that will help you write better copy:
https://neilpatel.com/blog/75-copywriting-resources/

Mittmaster Online martial arts education for students and instructors
mittmaster.com

THANK YOU FOR TAKING THE TIME TO READ MY BOOK.

I hope you found lots of actionable insights you can apply to your martial arts school.

If you need any help putting these principles into practice, I offer **1-1 coaching for martial arts instructors to help them grow their business**.

My **"On The M.A.T" coaching program** focuses on three key areas:

Motivation

Motivation is the foundation of success, but many instructors set goals that are too small. And small goals don't get you excited and energised every day.

Choosing, setting, and working towards LIFE CHANGING goals is where the magic happens.

The first step to changing your school (and your life) is to work out where you are, work out where you'd like to be, and formulate a plan of action to get you there

Accountability

I believe accountability is the key to success.

The problem with running your own show is that you are accountable to no one. If you procrastinate and scroll social media all day, no one will call you on it.

If you don't take consistent action toward your goals, no one is going to remind you of the commitment you made.

And if you say you'll do something and then don't, no one is going call you out on your inconsistency

This is why accountability is so important.

We all need to feel that someone has got our back but is also keeping us honest and focused on our goals

Training

Once you are motivated & accountable the third element you need is training.

Training is about bridging the gap between your skills and your goals.

Most instructors have great teaching & technical skills but often they lack sales, marketing & communication skills

If after reading that you feel like you'd benefit from 1-1 coaching, **please scan the QR code** below to learn more.

To your success

Matthew Chapman

https://www.mittmaster.com/

https://www.matthewchapman.online/

https://www.teachyourpassiononline.co.uk/

Printed in Great Britain
by Amazon

14950098R00133